HOW TO
BE BRIEF

BY RUDOLF FLESCH

THE ART OF CLEAR THINKING

THE ART OF PLAIN TALK

THE ART OF READABLE WRITING

THE BOOK OF UNUSUAL QUOTATIONS

HOW TO MAKE SENSE

HOW TO TEST READABILITY

HOW TO WRITE, SPEAK, AND THINK MORE EFFECTIVELY

A NEW WAY TO BETTER ENGLISH

WHY JOHNNY CAN'T READ—AND WHAT YOU CAN DO ABOUT IT

THE WAY TO WRITE (WITH A. H. LASS)

HOW TO
BE BRIEF;

AN INDEX TO SIMPLE WRITING

RUDOLF FLESCH

HARPER & ROW, PUBLISHERS

New York and Evanston

To Janet

This is a book to help you write brief, simple English.

Simple writing is hard. It's easy to write elaborate, long-winded sentences and paragraphs, express yourself like everybody else, use stiff, lifeless language. But it's hard to talk sense on paper, make the other fellow understand, be your natural self.

Keep this book on your desk and use it often. The secret of good writing is that you have a choice. At every point you can choose whether to use this word or that, write one sentence or two, say it one way or another. It's up to you to make the best choice.

Standard books on usage are not much help: they simply tell you what is conventionally or statistically approved. This book is different: it tells you, each time, what is practical, efficient and brief.

I arranged it alphabetically because that was the best way I could think of to give you quick, handy answers to your questions. Some of the entries give you better, shorter words (e.g. *frequently, lieu, require*), some give you rules on simple writing (e.g. *affixes, emphasis, present tense*), some deal with larger topics (e.g. *aphorisms, fables, magazines*). Please don't be disappointed if you come across an entry where I've listed only one type of synonym (e.g. *disposition, issue, sustain*) but none for other meanings of the word. I listed synonyms only for the word meanings I've found most common in pompous writing.

I hope you'll use this book not only as a reference book. Read it straight through from A to Z, browse in it, pick it up again from time to time. Keep it around. Simple writing isn't something you learn in a day or a week. It's a habit; it must slowly grow on you until it gets to be a way of life.

R. F.

HOW TO
BE BRIEF

A

a, an. Get rid of *a* and *an* whenever you can. There are three ways of doing this without falling into telegraphic, unnatural English: (1) you can use plurals instead of singulars (as in this sentence); (2) you can leave out the article before abstract and group nouns (e.g. *doubts arose; police arrested him*); (3) you can drop the article in certain idiomatic phrases (e.g. *fellow I met at lunch*). Go over your copy and try to kill every *a* and *an* in sight.

You can also go further and write in telegraphic style. You'll be amazed how easy it is to get used to this style in digests, summaries, condensations.

A, B and C. When you use an example or fictitious case, don't label the people *A*, *B* and *C*. Give them real-sounding names like Jones, Brown and Robinson.

abandon. Say *give up*.

abbreviations. In school and college they drummed into you that you mustn't use abbreviations in ordinary writing—too undignified. Nonsense. It's done all the time. Look at a page in *Time: U.S., circ., Ind., pop., W. Va., Jan., ft., in.,*

1

m.p.h. And everybody abbreviates middle names all the time. Go ahead and abbreviate whenever the spirit moves you.

To save even more space, leave out abbreviation periods whenever you can. The British omit them regularly after abbreviations that use the first and last letters, like *Mr, Mrs. Dr, St* (for Saint), *Thos, Chas, jr.* Periods are also often left out after standard abbreviations like *US, UN, FCC, PTA.* If you care to, you can go further and write *Kan, Jan, inc, av, rd, tel, Wed, co.*

If you want to use new, original abbreviations for extra space-saving, follow the pattern of most telephone books (e.g. *plmbg & heatg supls, atty, flrst, acctnts, svce, rl est*).

abide. *Abide by = stick to.*

abode. Sounds ridiculous. Say *house, address.*

abolish. Say *end.*

above. It's better to write *earlier, just, a moment ago.* Above shows your writing is meant to be read from a page, rather than a record of something said. Avoid all words that destroy the illusion of talk. Refer to time instead of space.

absence. Don't use *in the absence of* as a preposition. Say *without, since there's no,* etc.

absent. Means not there.

absolute constructions. *The meeting over, he immediately went to the airport.* This construction comes straight from the Latin, where it was used with the famous ablative absolute case. It's strictly formal English and wouldn't occur to anybody in ordinary conversation. Avoid it; if you want to save words, do something else.

absolutely. Usually unnecessary. Leave out.

absorb. *Take in, merge.*

abstain. *He abstained from voting = he didn't vote.*

abstract words. Sometimes they're necessary, but more often than not they're used without thinking, just cluttering up your sentences—nouns ending in *-tion, -ance* and *-osity,* adjectives ending in *-ive* and *-al,* verbs ending in *-ate,* etc. A special nuisance are compound prepositions and conjunctions, e.g. *with reference to, in connection with, pursuant to.*

Try to use as few abstract words as you can. Replace them with simple root words like *link* for *connection* or *size* for *dimension.* Usually, but not always, the replacement words will come from Saxon rather than Latin. It's also a good rule of thumb to use simple one-syllable verbs that mean movements of the human body; combined with adverbs, these verbs can do almost all the work usually done by abstract words. Examples: *condescension—look down on; disintegration—fall apart; intervention—come between; reminiscence—look back; dependence—lean on.*

Here's a list of the most useful 50 verbs and 20 adverbs:

VERBS			ADVERBS	
bear	go	slip	about	forth
blow	hang	split	across	in
break	hold	stand	ahead	off
bring	keep	stay	along	on
call	lay	stick	apart	out
carry	let	strike	around	over
cast	look	take	aside	through
catch	make	talk	away	together
come	pick	tear	back	under
cut	pull	throw	down	up
do	push	tie		
draw	put	touch		

3

VERBS			ADVERBS
drive	run	turn	
drop	set	walk	
fall	shake	wear	
get	show	work	
give	skip		

abstracts. An abstract is a brief summary of the main points. Cut away everything that's unessential; then translate the rest into brief simple language.

abundance. *Lots (of).*

accept. *Take.*

accidentally. *By chance, by mistake.*

accompany. Say *go with, be with.*

accomplish. Fancy word for *do.*

accordance. Avoid the preposition *in accordance with.* Try *by* or *under.*

according to. Again, try *by* or *under.* Or rewrite.

accordingly. How about *so?*

account. *On account of = because of, due to.*

accuracy. Journalism students are taught that accuracy comes first—"Spell the names right!" That's true for all writing. Accuracy also improves your style: it forces you to pay attention to details and get away from fancy, vague writing. As long as you're bound to mention names, ages, addresses, and quote verbatim what people said, you can't help being simple and clear. Specify, be accurate, give exact details—and forget about fine writing and original style.

accusation. *Charge.*

achieve. Fancy word for *reach, get.*

acknowledgment. It's traditional to start a business letter

4

acknowledgment (*Contd.*)

with the acknowledgment of the incoming letter. Don't. The opening sentence of your letter is its show window; use it to tell the addressee the most important thing he ought to know. Start with what newspapermen call a summary lead and tell the gist of your story right away. Don't write *Thank you very much for your letter of February 19, 1962, in which you . . .*; write *Here's your check for $239.65.*

If you feel you *have* to acknowledge the other letter some-where, do it inconspicuously at the tail end of your first sen-tence, e.g. *Here's your check for $239.65—the refund you asked for in your letter of February 19.* Or better still, put such clerical details in a caption, away from the main body of your letter.

acquainted. *Be acquainted with = know.*

acquire. Whats' wrong with *get?*

active voice. The active voice is always better than the passive. Don't argue; don't come up with such famous excep-tions as *Smith was murdered.* That's no excuse for writing *Your suggestion was carefully studied by the committee and given every consideration.*

addition. Don't use *in addition* as a conjunction; say *then* or go right on with your next thought. Don't use *in addition to* as a preposition; say *aside from* or recast the sentence and say *and.*

address. Addresses add to readability. A *lady in Ohio* sounds more like a real person than just *a lady; Mrs. Roger P. Scott, of 24 Cherry Lane, Pottstown, Neb.* is far more con-vincing than *Mrs. Roger P. Scott* of nowhere.

adequate. Say *enough, good.*

adjacent. *Nearby. Adjacent to = next to.*

adjectives. Adjectives are words that describe persons or

5

things by qualities they have in common with other persons or things: an *attractive* brunette is compared to other attractive brunettes, a *compact* car is like other compact cars. Such generalizations weaken your style. Try to use as few adjectives as you can; do your describing with verbs and nouns. Homer described the beauty of Helen of Troy by telling what the sight of her did to some old men.

adjust, adjustment. Fashionable terms of psychology and education. It's clearer and simpler to say *sane, doing well,* etc.

administer. Try *run, manage, handle.*

administration. *Rule, handling.*

advance. Try *rise, go up, get ahead.*

advantageous. Long word for *good.*

adverbs. Adverbs are like adjectives, only they modify verbs rather than nouns. They're just as weak as adjectives. Don't write *He replied softly;* write *I could hardly hear what he said.*

advertising. Tests prove that simple copy sells merchandise. Fancy prose does not; it may win awards or get talked about along Madison Avenue but the customers usually don't remember the name of the product.

advise. Business jargon for *write* or *tell.* Don't use it in that sense.

advisement. *Under advisement* is a euphemism for *no.* Don't use.

advocate. *He advocated = he was for.*

affect. Vague, formal word. Use *touch, hurt, bear on,* etc.

affirmative. *He gave an affirmative answer = he said yes.*

affixes. Affixes are prefixes and suffixes. The more prefixes and suffixes you use, the heavier and slower your writing.

6

affixes (*Contd.*)

Indigestibility has four affixes: the prefixes *in-* and *di-* and the suffixes *-ibil* and *-ity*. (*-gest-* is the root or stem.) Words with affixes are invariably abstract. Cut down on them: figure out for yourself what you might say instead of *indigestibility*.

aforementioned, aforesaid. The simplest words to use instead are *this* and *that*. *I entered the aforementioned building at 8.45 a.m.* = *I entered this building at 8.45 a.m.* Often the article *the* will do: *I entered the building at 8.45 a.m.*

age. Ages, like addresses, add to realism. *Edgar M. Nussbaum, 67,* is more real than just *Edgar M. Nussbaum.*

agreement. Grammarians spend a lot of time telling you that nouns, pronouns and verbs must agree. If you say *everybody,* you mustn't say *they;* if you say *the company,* you mustn't say *them.* But idiomatic English doesn't always care about agreement, and it's a good idea to stick to idiom in your writing. If it seems natural to you to say *they* after *everybody* or *the company,* write it that way. *I complained to the company six weeks ago, but it didn't even answer my letter* is grammatically correct but doesn't sound like anything anyone would say.

aid(e). Headline writers dug up the rare word *aide* to use it for *employee* or *staff member.* After some years they decided to drop the final *e* and now every headlined jobholder is an *aid.* Forget that word; call a v.p. a v.p. and a clerk a clerk.

AIDA formula. Old standby of advertising and sales writing. It goes like this: (1) attention, (2) interest, (3) desire, (4) action. To organize a speech or piece of writing, start with arousing attention and interest, then create desire for your product or idea, then wind up by telling your reader or audience what to do. A basic, foolproof scheme.

ain't. A reverse status symbol. If you say *ain't,* you admit you're lower class.

Aside from that, *ain't* is a natural idiomatic solution of an awkward language problem: we have no short form for *am not* and *isn't,* so the spirit of the English language came up with *ain't.* Perhaps some time in the future people will be less status-conscious and *ain't* will be accepted.

alibi. *Alibi* is Latin and means *somewhere else.* Purists say you shouldn't use it to mean *excuse,* but don't worry about that.

all of. You don't need *of.*

allege. Legal jargon. Use *say.*

alleviate. Say *lighten* or *ease.*

allusions. Don't allude to things the reader may not be familiar with; it's tactless to use inside jokes or private language. And I don't mean just literary or classical allusions; they're rare nowadays, but allusions to sports or show business are common. Don't take it for granted that everyone watches Westerns or follows baseball. Some people even manage to escape commercials for deodorants.

along the lines of. You mean *like.*

alright. Webster (1961) says it's all right to spell it *alright.*

alteration. Means *change.*

alternative. A long word. *Choice* will usually do.

amount. *In the amount of:* say *of* or put the amount before the noun. *He had to pay a bill in the amount of $463.75 = he had to pay a $463.75 bill.*

ampersand. Just like abbreviations, the ampersand (&) is supposed to be undignified. Never mind. If you want to save space, use it. It's used throughout the most literary of all how-to-write books, Fowler's *Modern English Usage.*

and. As I just said, use & if you want to save space. Or use a comma, as in *Among those present were cabinet members, diplomats, other celebrities.*

Should you use a comma before *and* in a series? There are two schools of thought who have fought each other to a standstill. But it's clearly shorter and faster to leave out the comma, as in *meat, potatoes and vegetables.*

It's a superstition that you shouldn't start a sentence with *and.* Why not? Do it if you feel like it; but don't put a comma after the *and.*

and/or. Lawyers thought this up, and literary people have objected to it for decades. But they've never come up with a good substitute. *The murder was committed by Smith, Brown and/or Robinson* means that either Smith did it or Brown or Robinson or any two or all three of them together. *And/or* is the only way of saying this in one short word.

and which. Sentences with *and which* are usually cumbersome and often grammatically wrong. Steer clear of them.

anecdotes. Magazine articles have to be stuffed to the brim with anecdotes, or editors won't buy them. The principle is sound: illustrate facts and ideas with stories, incidents, cases, practical applications, funny sayings, entertaining tidbits, amusing sidelights, curious happenings—in short, anecdotes. They're the stuff of daily life.

angle. Overused word. Rewrite. *From the taxpayer's angle = for the taxpayer.*

Anglo-Saxon. Anglo-Saxon words are usually shorter and better than Romance words, but don't overdo it. Don't call a villain a knave.

answers. In ordinary conversation, answers are usually elliptical—that is, they leave out all words implied by the question. *Where did you go? Out. What did you do? Nothing.* Use the same technique in writing. Instead of *The peculiar advantage of this system is that it allows for speedy intake of the information involved* write *What makes this system so good? Speed.*

answers to complaints. When people complain, they're either right or wrong. When they're right, say so immediately and admit your mistake. When they're wrong, don't give them the brushoff but start your answer by showing that you understand what's bothering them. Then lead up to your refusal by giving good reasons for your stand.

answers to requests. When people ask for something and your answer is yes, say so in the opening sentence. When your answer is no, it's also better to come right out with it and say you're sorry you can't give them what they want. Only when the request was well-founded and your refusal will be a real disappointment, soften the blow and start with your reasons for saying no.

anticipate. Misused as long variant for *expect*. The stock joke is the phrase *anticipating marriage*, which literally means premarital sex.

anxiety. Fashionable word for *fear*.

anyplace. If it comes to you naturally to say *anyplace* for *anywhere*, say *anyplace*.

aphorisms. An aphorism is a short, memorable saying. Scientific medicine, for instance, started with the aphorisms of Hippocrates, who used them to make his students remember the things he'd learned from experience. If you can coin an occasional aphorism, more power to you.

apology. Never be afraid to admit a mistake. People love

10

apology (*Contd.*)

to get letters from corporations and government agencies saying they're sorry.

apostrophes. Most apostrophes are used in contractions like *don't* and possessives like *Joe's*. Since both are devices for brevity, apostrophes are a sure sign of an effective, fast style.

Apostrophes are also used in words like *'way down, year 'round, the '30's*, etc. The trend is to leave them out and write *way down, year round, the 30s*.

apparent. Try *clear, plain*.

appear. If something is so, don't say it appears to be so. Don't hedge: if the customer hasn't paid the last instalment, don't write *It appears that we never received your payment*.

applicable. Rewrite. Try *fits, can be used by, is good for, is for, works*.

apply. *Fit, bear on, hold, be good for, work*.

apposition. Don't cram appositions into your sentences. Don't write *A Sunday painter, he is also interested in books and music*. Write *He is a Sunday painter and also interested in books and music*.

appreciate. Overused as a long variant for *thanks*. Try to write without using *appreciate* once. It's hard but it can be done.

appropriate. Means *proper*.

approximately. Say *about*.

apt to. Shorter than *likely* or *liable to*. Never mind the fine distinction some people insist on.

area. Generally used when people want to be vague. *We have conducted a certain amount of research in this area* comes as close to saying nothing as anything can get.

aren't. Look at the words *are not* in the sentence you've just written. Wouldn't *aren't* be better?

argument. It's nice to raise an argument and present it convincingly. But is it necessary? Will your reader be interested? Will he learn something he ought to know? Aren't you just satisfying your ego by going into all this?

arise. Don't use *arise* as a synonym for *get up*. On second thought, don't use it at all. *The question arose = someone asked.*

arithmetic. Don't give your reader bits of arithmetic in the middle of a paragraph. If you want to tell him he has to pay $6.24 plus 50 cents handling charges plus 43 cents postage, totaling $7.17, show him the addition in a neat little vertical table, the way he's used to seeing it.

armchair thinking. Psychologists have shown that isolation does something bad to your mental processes. Armchair thinking is bad because it gets you away from facts and other people's ideas. Get out of that armchair and do some legwork: it'll improve your style.

arrangement. An empty word. *The arrangement was that we should meet at 5 p.m. = We were to meet at 5 p.m.*

art criticism. Don't be pompous. Don't tell people what they ought to feel.

articles. Articles, in contrast to essays, are based on facts and research. When you write an article, don't try to substitute an essay based on your own opinions.

articles (grammar). Be relentless in cutting out *a, an* and *the*.

as. The conjunction *as* is a pet of reporters trying to tell everything in the lead sentence. *Rinaldo Ruatti, of Italy, sent here as a replacement for retired world champion Eugenio Monti, yesterday stunned experts as he rocketed to the world two-man bobsled title and a track record. . . . A wealthy*

12

as (*Contd.*)

Nassau County, L.I., lawyer died today with his wife and young son as he tried to lead them from their burning home in Old Brookville after he had ushered his daughter to safety.
Don't glue your sentences together with *as*. Two sentences are better than one.

as ever. Good ending for a letter to a friend or close associate (others are *yours* or *ever yours*). Use these informal endings whenever they feel right.

as such. Leave out.

as to. All-purpose preposition that adds to vagueness. Use the exact preposition instead. Better still, recast the sentence: *As to the question of inheritance taxes, I would advise that* . . . = *I advise you to do such-and-such to save inheritance tax.*

as to whether. *The question as to whether* = *the question whether; doubt as to whether* = *doubt whether; discussion as to whether* = *discussion whether.*

ascertain. Why not *make sure* or *find out?*

aspect. You mean *side.*

assert. Means *say* or *claim.*

assist. *Help.*

associated with. A grand phrase for saying you have a job with the XYZ company—a minor job, because otherwise you'd say what it is.

assume. There are only a few rare occasions when *assume* is better than *think.*

asterisk. The U. S. Government Style Manual calls for asterisks to show that part of a quotation has been left out. Everyone else uses three dots.

attached please find. Old-fashioned business jargon. Don't even say *attached is* or *enclosed is;* say *here's.*

13

attain. Try *reach, get, win, make.*

attempt. Say *try.*

attend. When someone attends a meeting or party, it means he's there.

attention. *It was brought to my attention* = normally I wouldn't be bothered with such trifling matters, but one of my underlings dared to disturb me with this.

attributable. *Due.*

attribution. Newspapers have to be careful to attribute the news to its source: *There will be no war this year, an authoritative source in the State Department said today.* I suppose this is necessary, but it makes for awkward sentence endings in almost everything you read in the paper.

augment. Try *raise, add to.*

author's pride. The greatest obstacle to good writing. H. L. Mencken used to say he never once in his life objected to an editor's changes in his copy. Follow his example.

average. The average is always mythical, but it's an unbeatable way to tell quickly what's in a mass of figures. Always give readers the average and the range.

avail. *Avail yourself of* = *use. Of no avail* = *no use.*

aware. To be *aware* is to *know.*

B

background. If you *have* to tell about the past history of the thing you're writing about, leave it till later. Start with what's interesting *now.*

bad habits. Every writer has certain bad habits, like over-using *very, obviously, particularly, in other words.* What are yours? Try to get rid of them.

balance. Used universally in the U.S. to mean the remainder.

bar. Headline word for *shut out.* Don't use.

basis. One of those meaningless words you better avoid. *On the basis of last year's earnings, this figure represents* 116% = this is 116% of last year's earnings.

be. All forms of the verb to be—*is, are, was, were*—are signs that you probably used a weak passive voice or *be*-with-noun construction. Hunt for a strong active verb and rewrite.

beginnings. Start whatever you write—letter, memo, report, article—with a newspaper-type lead. Put first things first. Tell the reader right off what he'd want to know most. Answer the question on top of his mind. Spill the beans.

behavior pattern. Psychological jargon for the way people act.

belongingness. More psychological jargon.

below. Don't refer to space; refer to time. Don't say *below:* say *later.*

beneficial. Long word for *good.*

bestow. Means *give.*

better. People write *you had better,* but don't say it. They say *You better look into this right away.* Write it *you'd better* or, if you dare, *you better.*

between you and I. Don't upset people by saying *between you and* I. Say *between you and me*—it doesn't cost anything to be idiomatic *and* grammatical.

beverage. Ever heard anyone use the word *beverage* in conversation? Say *drink.*

15

Bible. The King James Version is still the most glorious collection of good strong English there is. Read the newer versions and compare.

bid. A headline word—otherwise used only in bridge.

biography. Disraeli said, "Read no history, only biography, for that is life without theory." *Write* no history either, only biography, for that is what interests people.

boldface. In newsletters, bulletins, etc., put the lead sentence of each item in boldface—gives the reader a chance to pick the items from the page in one quick glance.

bona fide. Why use Latin? Say *genuine, real.*

book reading. Don't let your book reading show through your writing. Don't write a patchwork quilt of *As Dr. Jones put it. . . . as Bertram Robinson says . . . as Wilberforce remarks . . . as Martin S. Zimmerman put it . . . as Prof. Scholzhammer notes . . .*

boxes. A black line around anything in print makes it stand out; gives the reader the feeling that here's something special.

bracket. Don't write about socio-economic brackets, write about people.

brainstorming. There's a theory that a dozen people around a table will produce good ideas by not thinking, just shooting their mouths off freely. One man doing his legwork will do better.

brevity. Samuel Butler said, "Brevity is not only the soul of wit but the soul of making oneself agreeable, and of getting on with people, and indeed of everything that makes life worth having."

brushoff. Never give people the brushoff. There's no way of covering it up and making people feel they're *not* getting

16

the brushoff when they are. Treat them nicely and try to understand how they feel.

business English. In the 1800s shopkeepers had to write occasional letters to their wealthy patrons. They thought a mixture of humble phrases and pseudo-refined language would sit well with them. And that's how we got *your goodselves, your favor has come to hand,* and *we beg to remain.*

but. If you feel like starting a sentence with *but,* start it with *but.* But don't put a comma after it.

buttonholing. There's nothing quite as effective as reaching out from the page and talking to your reader directly. *Six babies have been brought into the world during the time it took you to read this sentence*—that sort of thing.

C

call. A handy word. Example: *Let's call him Jim Taylor* (because that is not his name).

can and may. You've heard about this since grammar school days—*can* for ability, *may* for permission. But most people don't care about this distinction and say things like *The law says you can do that.* Be idiomatic: use *can* for permission too.

can't, couldn't. Use contractions.

capitals. It's good to use many words with capitals in your writing, because that means you've mentioned names, dates, places—you're dealing with understandable specifics instead of vague generalities. But don't just slap capitals onto any common noun that you think will look better that way; the down style (*street, ave., govt.*) reads faster than the up style.

Don't put headlines and titles in all caps but make them caps and lower case: it's easier on the reader's eyes and makes for faster reading.

captioned. Don't say *the captioned account.* Say *this account.*

captions. Picture captions cry out for the telegraphic style. Example from *Time: Archipenko's The Boxers is cubist abstraction suggesting free-swinging action.*

case. Meaningless all-purpose word that can easily be spared. *In this case = here. In case = if. This is not the case = it isn't so. In the case of New Jersey commuters = for New Jersey commuters.*

case history. Medical case histories are usually fine examples of terse, concrete English. *Patient suffers from frequent headaches. Temperature 101. Complains of pain in the left arm. . . .*

category. *Class* is shorter.

cause. Sounds bookish. Try *bring, bring on, make, make for.*

cease. Say *stop.*

celebrate. Try *keep, mark.*

charts. By all means show things visually with charts and diagrams. But don't expect them to speak for themselves. Explain them; show what they show.

checklist. Nothing beats a checklist for sheer readability. It breaks the material down into bite-size chunks and gives readers something to do with a pencil. There's no better way to make them take in what you said.

children's books. Good children's books are written by

18

people who love children and can tell them stories on paper; bad children's books are written by hacks working within a controlled vocabulary. The secret of what appeals to children lies not in the "familiar" words but in the spirit of fun, adventure and excitement. If the child runs across a word he's never seen before, so much the better; where else should he learn it?

chronology. It's good to start with an exciting lead, then go back and tell your story from the beginning, the way it happened. Write so the reader will ask what happened next.

circumstances. There's nothing wrong with *under the circumstances*; only fusspots insist on *in the circumstances*. But it's better to avoid the long word *circumstances* altogether and write something like *what with all that, as it is.*

claim. Useful short American idiom for *assert, maintain, state.*

clauses. Sentences can have independent clauses (that can stand alone) and subordinate clauses (that can't). Subordinate clauses make for heavy writing, weighed down with complex sentences. Split your sentences up; turn subordinate clauses into separate sentences; use more periods, semicolons and colons.

clearing your throat. Most people write a paragraph or two or three before they're warmed up to their subject. Cross it out. Start where you start *talking.*

clichés. Textbooks warn against clichés, but few people mind them. If a cliché expresses best what you want to say, use it. The substitute may make you sound pompous.

climate. *The intellectual climate . . . the political climate . . . the climate of opinion.* Fashionable phrases, but what exactly do they mean? Rewrite.

clipped words. Don't call *laboratory, mathematics* and

examination what your readers are used to calling *lab, math* and *exam.* Call a *phone* a *phone;* call *TV TV.*

close. Don't use *close* as a more elegant substitute for *shut.*

cognizant. *I am cognizant of* = *I know.*

coherence. Aristotle said a piece of writing must have unity, coherence and emphasis. Don't try to produce coherence artificially by tying every sentence and paragraph to the preceding one by some connective or transitional device. Don't write a never-ending succession of *moreover, furthermore, nevertheless, in addition.* Write it tight. See to it that your facts and ideas follow each other naturally so that coherence will come by itself.

coincidentally. *At the same time.*

collection letters. Collection letter experts learned long ago that you have to take the world as it is. Don't write mechanically your first, second and third letter and then pass the matter on to your lawyer; write with a feeling for people's troubles and frustrations. Try to get an answer from them; show them you want to help; offer a way out. They'll respond if they sense a human being at your end.

colloquial. *Colloquial* has to do with the spoken language. By all means write colloquially, the way you talk. Writing is a record of speech, there's no getting away from it. Don't worry about *colloquial* meaning *slang;* it doesn't. Don't be a different person on paper.

colon. Learn to write with lots of colons. Semicolons and colons are the right marks between shorter independent sentences; they show that two ideas belong together. The colon does a special job: it signals to the reader that the next sentence will fulfill what the last one promised (as in this example).

colon (*Contd.*)

Don't use a capital after a colon when you use it that way.

Remember to use a colon whenever you're tempted to write *thus, namely, in other words, the result is that.*

Use a comma—not a colon—before direct quotes, e.g. *He said,* "OK."

color. Don't strain for colorful writing. If something is quaint, or gory, or vividly dramatic, tell it so the reader will discover this for himself.

comma. There's a trend toward using as few commas as possible. Once it was taught that all adverbial words and phrases had to be surrounded by commas. Not any more. It used to be correct to write *Therefore, Smith, today, was, suddenly, fired;* now it's *Therefore Smith today was suddenly fired.*

When in doubt, leave it out.

comma fault. English teachers frown on what they call the comma fault—a comma used instead of a period. But often the so-called comma fault isn't a fault at all. *He ripped open the letter, he was so excited* is perfect English; so is *I went back downtown, I'd forgotten the groceries.*

commence. Too bookish; say *start* or *begin.*

comment. *He commented* = *he said.*

communicate, communication. Fashionable words, vastly overused. Don't *communicate—write, phone, tell, keep in touch, contact, send a greeting card.*

community. What kind of community? Is it a city, a town, a village, a suburb? Call it what it's called.

compare, comparison. Try *match, matching.*

compatible. *Matching, fitting.*

compel. Say *force, make.*

compensation. Usually means *pay.*

complaints. When a complaint is justified, say you're sorry. When it isn't, explain why.

When you're the one who's making a complaint, be specific about what went wrong. Give the facts; don't foam at the mouth.

complete. Don't tell people to *complete this form*; tell them to *fill out the blank*.

complex words and sentences. Complex sentences have one or more subordinate clauses; complex words have one or more affixes (e.g. *interdenominational*). Use few complex words and sentences; replace them by simple ones. This is the main secret of clear writing.

complimentary close. Don't end your letter with

Hoping to hear from you soon, I remain,

Very truly yours,

End your letter with a period: *We hope to hear from you soon.* Nothing sounds quite as old-fashioned as *we are* or *we remain*.

comply. A formal, legalistic word. Instead of *comply with the rules* say *follow the rules*. Instead of *you are asked to comply* say *please do this*.

composition. In the Middle Ages, when schools taught only Latin and Greek, students were taught to write compositions in those languages. Then, when courses in Englist started, they had to write English compositions too. Which is why to this day we write school themes and essays and other exercises in putting our own language on paper. Does that prepare us for real-life writing jobs? It does not. Once we're out of school, nobody ever asks us to write themes or essays; instead we have to write reports, letters, memos, press releases, contributions to trade papers. If we keep on writing compositions, we're lost.

compound. A compound sentence consists of two or more independent parts, e.g. *I opened the book and started the first chapter.* A compound word consists of two or more independent parts, e.g. *beanpole, haystack, catnip.* New compound words are being formed every day. Often they're not written or printed together but with white space in between, like *high school, sports car, divorce court, watch band, crash program.* (What makes them compounds is the accent on the first part.)

Hyphens in compounds are on the way out. Fifty years ago people wrote *to-day*; now it's *today.* When in doubt, leave the hyphen out and write it either together (like *fallout*) or separately (like *stock option*).

If you want to be brief, use lots of compounds.

comprise. *Have* will often do: *This town comprises five election districts* = *this town has five election districts.*

conceal. Say *hide.*

concept. Don't use *concept* as a fancy synonym for *idea.*

concerned. Usually unnecessary. *As far as the budget is concerned, we must remember that it is . . .* = *we must remember the budget is . . . .*

concerning. Long preposition. Say *on, about.*

concise. There's a difference between being concise and being brief. You may be concise (by using a few highly condensed words) without being brief; it costs the reader more time to push through a small thicket of words than to walk through a longer sentence.

conclude. A formal word. Why not *think?* Or *figure?* And for the other meaning of *conclude*, why not *wind up?*

conclusion. The rule of thumb for the conclusion of a letter, report, article is to tell the reader what to do. If it's something concrete and specific like mailing a coupon or writing a check, fine; if it isn't, tell him at least to remember, to keep in mind, think about, come in again, let us know. Don't say *don't hesitate to call upon us if we can be of any further help*: it's old-fashioned.

concrete. A concrete word means something you can point to or describe; that can be scientifically measured and analyzed; that has a word for it in any language. *Typewriter* is concrete; *gentleman* is not. Stick to concrete words in your writing and you can't go far wrong.

conflagration. A fire.

conformity. Don't be afraid of conformity in your writing. Write so that everybody understands what you mean; don't be a nonconformist in your style.

congratulations. Make your congratulations—like your condolences—specific. Write something that would fit no one else. Show you know what happened last year, or why he got the new job.

conjecture. Means *guess.*

conjunctions. Stick to simple conjunctions rather than complex or compound ones. Write *and, so, but, since, if, when, then, how, why;* don't write *furthermore, nevertheless, consequently, for the reason that, in the event that, at the time when, thereupon, in this manner, for what purpose, in lieu of, taking into consideration the fact that.*

connected with. Like *associated with,* means you're *employed by.*

connection. *Link, tie.* And don't use the lazy man's conjunction *in connection with. In connection with the difficulties of daily commuting, many people complain = many people complain of the troubles of daily commuting.*

connectives. Replace heavy connectives with light ones.

24

connectives (*Contd.*)

Better still, keep an even flow of ideas that needs no connectives at all.

consensus. Everybody thinks so.

consequently. *So.*

consider. Means *think* or *look at.*

considerable. Long word for *large.*

consideration. Favorite word for polite brushoffs. *We have given your suggestion serious consideration* = it's no good.

constitute. *Form, make up, be. This constitutes a real danger* = *this is a real danger.*

consult. Fancy word for *ask.*

consummate. Try *utmost, top.*

contact. English teachers are against *contact* as a verb, but what else can you use for write-or-phone? *Get in touch* is too long.

contain. *Have. What does it contain?* = *What's in it?*

contemplate. Long, pompous word for *think about. He contemplated having a drink before going home* = *he thought he might have one.*

continue. *Stay, keep, keep on.*

contractions. Words like *don't, it's, haven't, you'll, we'd, that's, won't* are the chief tool of the writer who wants to be brief. They save not only space, they also set an informal tone. They are a must. It's hard to be pompous when you're using contractions.

contribute. Try *give, add to.*

convenience. *At your earliest convenience* = *as soon as you can.*

conversation. Face-to-face talk is the basic form of human communication. Language means talk—not speech-making or writing, but questions and answers, story-telling, give-and-take, interruptions, chatter. The mark of good writing is the feel of conversation with reader.

cookbook style. There's nothing better for direct instruction. Take this; do that; let simmer. You can't go wrong as long as you follow the pattern.

cooperate. *Please cooperate with us = please help us.*

copy. Are all these copies necessary? How about jotting down a memo without a copy? Must the files always bulge?

cordially. Someone had the bright idea that there ought to be a friendlier ending for business letters than *yours truly* or *yours sincerely*; so he invented *cordially*, and the word stuck. It still sounds phony and artificial. It's not the word you'd use in writing to a friend, is it?

corny. It's better to be corny than pompous.

corporate writing. In a corporation, the writer is usually not the same as the signer. This makes for a nervous, mumbling style—will he sign this?—and stifles all forceful expression.

correct. Try *right, true.*

correct grammar. Modern grammarians insist there's no such thing as correct grammar: whatever is widely used is acceptable. But that doesn't help those who feel that correct grammar is needed for better jobs; they want the traditional thing even if it isn't scientific. Luckily, you can be informal and colloquial and still 100% correct in your grammar; you don't have to say *ain't* to be brief.

course. Often unnecessary. *In the course of the investigation = during the investigation.*

courtesy. Don't sacrifice courtesy for brevity. When brevity is apt to sound abrupt and offensive, take more time.

create, creative. Overused. God created the world; don't

create, creative (*Contd.*)

use the same word for thinking up hairdos, desserts, popular songs.

credit letters. Credit letters have a language of their own. *This valued customer has an account of large proportions . . .* The credit man at the other end will know how to translate. There's no point in tampering with the code.

criterion. Fancy word meaning *standard*. Rewrite. *We applied geographic and economic criteria = we wondered where to put it and how much it would cost.*

culinary. Fancy word to use in the kitchen.

cutting. There's hardly anything written that can't be improved by cutting. When in doubt, cut it out.

D

dangling participle. *Spending an hour inside the store, the weather suddenly turned cold and nasty.* That's a dangling participle: it wasn't the weather that spent an hour in the store, it was you. Avoid long, complex sentences that start with participial phrases, and you'll be less apt to fall into this trap.

dare say. Bookish phrase. Skip it.

dash. Whenever you'd pause in the middle of a sentence, use a dash. Learn to use it; it's one of the handiest punctuation marks you've got.

Never use a comma with a dash—the dash is all you need.

data. Why use a Latin word? Say *facts, figures, statistics—* whatever you have.

dates. Dates make good reading. Tell when it happened; fix the event on the clock and the calendar. *He died at 9 p.m. on Sunday, January 28, 1962* says it better than *later on he died.*

Say 62 instead of 1962, whenever you can. It's shorter.

dearth. *Due to the dearth of* = *since there's no.*

deceased. Say *dead.*

declare. *He declared* = *he said.*

decline. Means *turn down.*

decrease. Say *cut, fall, drop, go down.*

deduct. *Take off, take away.*

deem. Much too formal for everyday use. Say *think.*

defer. Say *put off.*

deficiency. Something missing.

deficient. *Poor.*

defunct. *Dead.*

demonstrate. Say *show.*

density. Complex sentences filled with complex words make for density. There's no point in making it short if it's so condensed no one can read it.

departments. Use departments so the reader will know how to find his way around your publication. Don't surprise him with a new arrangement in every issue; make sure he'll be able to find his favorite items blindfolded. Familiarity is comfortable; there's no time-saver like having everything handy in a fixed place.

deprivation. Means *loss.*

deprive. *Take away.*

derive. *Get* will usually do.

descend, descent. *Go down, come down.*

description. Don't waste time with descriptions like a Victorian novelist. Get down to business fast.

desideratum. Fancy word for *wish, aim, goal.*

designation. *Name, label.*

desire. Make it *wish* or *want.*

destination. Write *aim, goal.*

details. The more details you give, the clearer it will be, the livelier, the more interesting. But don't bore the reader by telling him what the weather was like when the company was founded and the names of all the ushers at the wedding.

deteriorate. *Get worse, run down.*

determine. Means sometimes *fix, set* or *settle,* sometimes *find out* or *figure out. Is determined by = hinges on, turns on, depends on.*

detrimental. *Bad, harmful.*

develop. *What developed next = what happened next.*

dialogue. Professional writers use lots of dialogue. Tell as much of your story as you can in real-sounding, lifelike dialogue. Even if you can't conjure up a couple of characters talking to each other, write in the form of a dialogue with your reader.

dichotomy. Fashionable long word. Means *split.*

dictation. Dictating a letter or memo instead of writing it usually makes it wordier and less concise. There ought to be an advantage because it's talked out instead of written down, but dictating isn't the same thing as talking freely to someone else. The typical dictated letter sounds even more formal than one that's put on paper directly.

dictionaries. Older dictionaries start their definitions with the word's historical meaning, which is often obsolete; newer dictionaries tell right away what it means now, usually in the simplest way. Use a newer dictionary to find simple synonyms for the heavy items in your vocabulary.

different than. Some people insist you should say *different from* instead of *different than*. But why change *You look different than you used to?* There's no better way of saying it.

difficulty. Don't use as a synonym for *trouble*.

digests. Scientific or legal digests give the essence for the professional reader; popular digests focus on readable nuggets, lively tidbits and anecdotes. Be sure you know what you're trying to do when you digest.

Don't be afraid to translate into colloquial English.

dignity. Don't try to preserve your dignity at all costs. Unbend; be your natural self; let your dignity take care of itself.

digressions. If you want to be brief, you mustn't digress. But remember that the world's great literature is filled with digressions. Shakespeare's fools are always on hand to break the tension. Entertain people with digressions, and they'll love you.

dimension. *Size. Of large dimensions = big.*

direct approach. When you're all snarled up not knowing how to say it to your reader, try the direct approach. Say something like *Now I want to take up such-and-such. This is hard to explain, but I'll try. Suppose you . . .* etc.

directions for the reader. One of the secrets of effective writing is to tell the reader exactly what to do while reading. *Remember this; keep in mind that; don't forget the other. Be sure to; take note of; before you go on, think back; let me repeat.* Tell him what to watch out for, what to read fast, what to commit to memory. Tell him what you're going to tell him; then tell him; then tell him what you've told him.

directive. An *order*.

disadvantage. *Drawback*.

disclose. Usually means nothing more exciting than *show*. A *survey of our records disclosed* = we checked.

discontinue. *Stop*.

discover. Say *find*.

discovery. Everything these days is a breakthrough or discovery. Dental breakthrough: a new toothpaste; breakfast discovery: a new cereal.

discrepancy. Means *difference, gap*.

discretion. *At your discretion—free, open, up to you*.

disposition. What one does.

distribute. *Spread, share*.

do. *Do* is a "pro-verb" that can be used instead of a verb just as a pronoun can be used instead of a noun. *Do you solemnly swear? I do.* Handy for brief writing.

dodging. Dodging responsibility and buck-passing are the chief reasons for vague, unclear writing. Instead of saying yes or no, people write so that it's impossible to tell who said what.—Don't hedge; don't dodge.

don and doff. Two bookish words nobody ever *says*.

donate. Means *give*.

donation. Sounds like more than a *gift*, but isn't.

don't, doesn't, didn't. Contract these words whenever you'd contract them in speaking.

He don't is not a mistake but a colloquial form of *he doesn't*. However, like *ain't*, it's now a reverse status symbol and can't be used.

Don't hesitate to call on us. Overused. Rewrite.

don't know. The Talmud says, "Teach thy tongue to say 'I don't know.'" Always confess ignorance.

dots. Use three dots to mark omissions in your quotes and add a period to let an occasional sentence trail off. There's so much that can be done with good punctuation. . . .

double negative. In English you're not supposed to use a double negative. That doesn't stop people from saying *I haven't seen nobody,* but you mustn't write such things. Too bad—it wouldn't do no harm.

double-purpose writing. Don't try to do two things at once. Don't try to explain your specialty to a lay audience and earn the admiration of your colleagues at the same time.

Double-purpose writing never works.

dramatization. By all means dramatize what you have to tell, but be sure to do it right. Don't just go through your sentences mechanically and split them up into questions and answers. Dramatic dialogue should sound the way people talk.

due to. Handy idiomatic conjunction. Grammarians object to *the game was canceled due to rain,* but everybody says it.

duration. *Time* is shorter.

dwell. "*Where do you dwell?*" "*I dwell at 34 Maple Street.*" Nobody in the world talks like that.

dynamic. Means *forceful.*

dynamics. Fashionable word meaning how it works.

E

-eable. Spell it *-eable* when you need the *e* to show that the consonant is soft, as in *manageable, traceable.* But write *lovable, salable, likable, movable,* etc.

32

echelon. Fancy word for *rank*.

economical. Means *cheap*.

economy. Don't save space; save your reader's time. Anyone can switch from 10-point type to 6-point type and give readers eyestrain. But if you want to save readers' time, write so that their eyes race down the page, quickly taking in everything you've said.

edifice. Means *building*.

editing. The main part of a copy editor's job is cutting. Forestall him; edit your own copy; cut it to the bone.

editorial we. No matter how customary, the editorial *we* sounds pompous. When you speak for yourself alone, say *I*.

editorializing. Good newspapermen learn not to editorialize. Don't editorialize either in your reports, letters, articles. Did they ask you for your personal opinion? They didn't? Then keep it to yourself.

editorials. There's an old tradition that editorials have to be pontifical and a new tradition that they should be breezy. Figure out for yourself what readers prefer.

education. Education used to mean teaching children English, math, history, etc. and there was no call for a special language. Now they teach "not the subject but the child" and there's a new science of *skills, learnings, understandings* and *felt needs*.

educators. Good teachers would rather be called *teachers*.

effective. *Good, striking.*

effectuate. What does it mean in your sentence? *Start, work, use, get going?* Or don't you know?

elapse. Write *pass*.

elect. When it isn't Election Day, say *choose* or *pick*.

elegant variation. That's what Fowler (*Modern English*

33

Usage) called the use of fancy synonyms to avoid repetition. Example: *King Saud of Saudi Arabia moved from a four-room suite at the Peter Bent Brigham Hospital this week to forty rooms at the Sheraton Plaza Hotel. The monarch has been here since November 22 undergoing eye surgery and treatment for stomach ailment.* Why *the monarch* instead of *he?*

Whenever you feel the itch for elegant variation, use a pronoun instead. Write *King Saud moved . . . He has been here . . .* When you've used the pronoun four or five times, go back to the original word.

elementary. *Simple* is shorter.

elicit. Say *bring. This elicited a variety of responses = this brought various answers.*

eliminate. Say *cut, drop, leave out, throw out.*

ellipsis. When you use ellipsis in speech or writing, you leave out words that are understood without being said. It's what people do all the time when they're talking. *You busy? Got a moment? Heard the latest? He is? He can't be!*

If you want to be brief, use ellipsis. Cut every word you can spare.

embrace. Don't use *embrace* in the figurative sense. Say *cover, take in.*

emerge. Means *come out, get out, turn out.*

eminently. Say *highly.*

empathy. Fancy word meaning you know how other people feel.

emphasis. Use emphasis to make people better understand what you mean. Underline words and phrases you'd stress in speaking (in print, underlined words appear in italics). Give your readers the benefit of your raised voice. Theodore Roose-

34

velt used to underline a word or two in a letter before he signed it; made the recipient feel the President of the United States took a personal interest in his affairs.

You can also stress a word or phrase by putting it at the end of a sentence. When you write *Washington's worst traffic jam happened on the eve of Kennedy's inauguration,* you've stressed the inauguration; when you write *On the eve of Kennedy's inauguration Washington had its worst traffic jam,* you've stressed the traffic jam.

emphasize. *Stress* or *point up* is shorter.

employee manuals. Be sure to write in the "you" or cookbook style. Start with what they're getting and go on to say what they're supposed to do. Don't start off with the history of the company; put that way, way back.

empty words. Beware of empty words—words that could just as well be left out. Look twice at *case, fact, nature, character, matter,* etc.

enclosed please find. Say *here's.*

enclosures. Don't rely on enclosures to do your work for you. Don't say *You will find the information in the enclosed self-explanatory booklet;* tell them in your letter. If you must refer to a printed enclosure, be specific. Explain that the answer to such-and-such a question is at the bottom of page 4.

encounter. Fancy word for *meet.*

endeavor. Fancy word for *try.*

endings. The normal ending for almost anything you write should tell the reader what he should do, what all this means to him, what it adds up to. Recap; summarize; tie it all together in a neat package.

engage in. Don't *engage in* anything; *do* it.

enhance. *Raise, add to.*

ensue. *Follow.*

entail. Sometimes *entail* is the right word, but more often it's better to say *mean* or *call for.*

enthusiasm. Inspirational writers are all in favor of enthusiasm, but if you want brevity you mustn't get carried away. Check your enthusiasm; stick to the facts.

entire. Say *whole.*

entirety. *In its entirety* = all of it.

entity. A thing by itself; a *unit.*

envisage. *Predict, foresee, see, look for.*

enumeration. Whenever you can list things in 1, 2, 3 order, do so. Make it easy for your reader. But don't give him long, numbered lists of character traits or other intangibles; don't write A *good undertaker should be* 1. *self-reliant;* 2. *polite;* 3. *ambitious;* 4. *gregarious;* 5. *neat;* 6. *hard-working.*

equanimity. *Poise.*

equivalent. *Matching.*

-er. Write *theater, center, meter,* etc. Be modern.

erroneous. Say *wrong, mistaken.*

eschew. Strictly a legal word; say *avoid.* Don't say *shun* either: that's headline jargon.

espouse. Means *take up.*

essays. Essays have gone out of style; what you read in magazines are articles, based on research. Follow the trend; don't bore people with essays, based on what you think you know.

essence. The *gist, core, point.*

establish. *Set, settle, fix.*

establishment. *Setup.*

estimate. Try *guess* or *gauge.*

etc. It's shorter to write *etc.* than go on with the whole list. But it's even shorter to skip *etc.* too; usually you don't need it. If you write *This applies to farmers, businessmen, professionals, employees, housewives,* the reader doesn't need *etc.* to know it applies to fishermen too.

euphemism. Everybody uses euphemisms for words not used in polite society. But don't go overboard: write what you would *say.* You wouldn't say *my uncle succumbed last week,* would you?

event. *In the event that = if.*

eventually. *In the end.*

ever so. *Thank you ever so much* is too much. *Thank you very much* will do.

evidence. Don't use the verb *evidence* to mean *show. They evidenced great confusion = they showed great confusion.*

evidently. Usually means *I noticed.*

evince. Like *evidence,* means *show.*

exactness. Be exact. Give names, addresses, dates, measurements. How many, how often, at what time, for how much? If you have all that information, why not give it to your reader so he gets a clearer picture? And if you haven't got it, why didn't you get it? Don't write about anything without knowing all there is to know about it. (Yes, of course that's impossible; but at least you should have a guilty conscience if you haven't done all your homework.)

exaggeration. Don't exaggerate—except when it's natural and doesn't mislead. Readers won't mind if you write *That was the best meal I ever ate.*

examination. Say *exam, test, check, checkup.*

examine. Say *test, check, look into, study.*

examples. It doesn't pay to be brief if the thing isn't clear without an example or two. Take the time and space and show how it applies to Smith, Brown and Robinson and how it works out in dollars and cents.

exceed. *Go beyond, be more of.*

exceedingly. *Highly.*

exceptions. Rules are boring; exceptions are interesting. Tell about that sudden dip in the chart; the single case at the tail end of the distribution; the extraordinary case that defies all rules. The world will be fascinated by Liechtenstein and Monaco as long as those countries exist.

excessive. *Too much.*

excessively. *Too.*

exclamation points. They've become so rare they jump out at you in serious, factual writing. Why not use them from time to time? They work!

exclusively. Say *only.*

excuse. Never hesitate to apologize. When you've made a mistake, say so out loud.

execute. Try *do, make, sign.*

exercise care. Means *watch out.*

exhaustive. Say *full.*

existence. Rewrite and say *is* or *are.*

exorbitant. Try *huge, vast.*

expedite. Washington gobbledygook for *speed up.*

experience. *We regret that you experienced this difficulty* = *we're sorry you had trouble.*

experiment. Say *test.*

experimental. *Test* or *trial.*

explanation. An explanation is a rewording in terms familiar to your reader. Make sure you know what he knows and doesn't know; then go ahead and add to his knowledge. Meet him where he is. And don't use baby talk either—not

38

even when you're talking to children. They know a lot more than you think.

extend. Nowadays when people *extend* greetings, they usually say hello. Or hi.

extinguish. *Put out.*

eye. The verb is a headline word, as in ORBIT SHOT TEAM EYES HIGH SEAS. Avoid.

F

fables. Fables, tales, stories, parables are the finest ways of driving home a point. But don't forget that at the end of each of Aesop's fables he spelled out its moral. Illustrate what you mean to say; then point out the meaning of the illustration.

facetious. Many cumbersome polysyllabic words are used facetiously, with unspoken quotation marks. People will talk about *jocosity, nefariousnes, plethora, cacophony,* or *uxoriousness* with a faint smile. But gradually the smile fades away and those heavy-handed words have become a standard part of the vocabulary. Don't let that happen to you; don't use outworn polysyllabic humor in the first place. It isn't funny anyway.

facilitate. How about *help* or *make easy?*

facilities. Rewrite. (*Housekeeping facilities* = you can use the kitchen.) Or try *setup.*

fact. Often unnecessary. *Despite the fact that it was snowing hard* = *though it was snowing hard.*

factor. Empty word. *We must not overlook the political factor* = *we must not overlook politics.*

failure. Don't use words with negative meanings if you can help it. Instead of *due to his failure to, because of his lack of, in his absence* write *since he didn't, since he hadn't, since he wasn't there.* Always translate sentences with *failure: A fine will be imposed for failure to appear at the appointed time* = *if you're not there at the appointed time you'll be fined.*

false spokesman. Nothing is believable if it is said by the false spokesman. If you're an employer, don't pretend you're talking in the interest of the union; if you're white, don't act as if you were a Negro. People won't forget that you are what you are.

familiar words. School children are now taught to read by learning to recognize whole words. This has led to the notion that readability means using familiar words—words learned by children in the first few grades. Anyone who has ever tried to write within a controlled vocabulary knows better.

fatuous. Means *silly.*

feasible. It can be done.

favor. *In favor of* = *for.*

favorable. *Good. Favorable reply* = *yes.*

feelings. It's always good to express your feelings. Write *I'm sorry* when you're sorry; write *I'm glad* when you're glad. When you were pleasantly surprised, say *I was pleasantly surprised;* when you were highly embarrassed, say *I was highly embarrassed.* Whenever you feel anything toward the subject or the reader, put it on paper; readers will be grateful for the human touch.

Don't hurt your reader's feelings. Don't say *obviously* or *of course,* implying he was too dumb to notice; don't say *your*

40

failure to reply, accusing him of being unbusinesslike. Don't say *as everybody knows* if there's a chance he *doesn't* know and would feel ashamed of his ignorance.

fiction. Fiction is generally more readable than nonfiction. If you want to keep in touch with simple writing, read fiction.

fictitious names. Make them lifelike; make them sound like the names of real people.

field. Empty word. *In the social-science field = in social science.*

fillers. Most readers of the *Reader's Digest* turn first to the short items, jokes, quips. One-line jokes are more memorable than 1,000-page volumes.

finalize. The most notorious gobbledygook word. Avoid.

figures. Use figures whenever you can. *One in eight* says more than *many; 50 cents* says more than *a nominal fee.* Use percentages; give ages, addresses, dates. Mention the time of day.

Use numerals to save space. Printers usually spell out figures up to ten; but it's shorter to write 1 to 10. Round off whatever you can; say $3 instead of $2.98 unless the two-cent difference is important. Leave out zeros; write $5 *million* instead of $5,000,000.

filing. Don't let filing spoil your writing. If exact references are needed for filing, put them inconspicuously in a corner; don't fill the body of your letter or report with boring details.

finish. *I am finished = I am through.*

first names. By all means use first names whenever you'd use first names in speaking. Don't write to a man you call Joe as if you'd never seen him in your life. And keep the tone of your whole letter so the word *Joe* would fit in properly. *Considering the precariousness of the international situation* *at the present moment, it would appear to be imperative to.* . . . Now try this with Joe: *Considering the precariousness of the international situation at the present moment, Joe, it would appear to be imperative to.* . . . See what I mean?

five W's. Newspapermen are trained to get the five W's into their leads—who, what, when, where, why. (Sometimes they overdo it and stuff the five W's into one monster sentence.) The principle is sound: pay attention to the five W's in everything you write. Don't leave unanswered questions in your reader's mind.

flashbacks. Flashbacks are now standard technique for short stories and novels. The author opens with a dramatic scene and then flashes back to the beginning of the story. The standard newspaper report too is told by flashback: the lead tells what happened today and is followed by the background story. Learn to use flashbacks in most of your writing.

flow. A good public speaker talks to his audience in one uninterrupted flow; a poor one sticks to his prepared notes. In the same way, a good writer talks to his readers in an easy flow; a poor one puts words on paper by fits and starts. Learn to write without thinking of the mechanics; do it automatically, like driving a car. Don't compose a piece of writing: talk to your reader.

focus. Problems are solved by focusing on a key element of the situation; writing problems are solved the same way. Go over the material you're going to write about and focus on the key element that'll make the reader understand the whole thing. Sometimes that key element is not easy to spot; sometimes it can't be seen without looking at the matter from the reader's point of view. Anyway, don't start writing until

focus (*Contd.*)

you've found the proper focus; once you've found it, it's easy; without it, nothing seems to make sense.

folktales. Folktales have been told since time immemorial, the world over. They're all variations on the same plots—the basic vocabulary of world literature. Each of the plots is carefully designed to teach people the elements of moral, intelligent behavior.

Learn from folktales. If you want to teach people a lesson, tell them stories.

folksy. Don't try to be folksy. Be yourself.

following. Don't use *following* as a preposition meaning *after*.

footnotes. Footnotes are a nuisance. If you can get along without footnotes, by all means do so; if you have to have them, arrange them so the reader can go through the text without being bothered by the little numbers and tugged at by the small-print stuff at the bottom of the page. The best way is to put all footnotes at the end of the article or book and make the reference numbers as inconspicuous as possible. Some book authors get along without any reference numbers at all and refer back to the text by page numbers and key words. It's a good system.

Another good system is to put your references in parentheses right along with the text (e.g. Flesch, *Book of Unusual Quotations*, p. 93).

for. The preposition *for* is a harmless, everyday word, but the conjunction *for* is stately and bookish: *I was absent from school yesterday for I had a sore throat.* Say *since* or *because*.

for the purpose of. *For* is enough.

for the reason that. Say *because*.

for your information. Of course. Why say so?

43

foreign words. Beware of foreign words. If your reader doesn't know the word, he'll feel uncomfortable; if he does, he may know more about it than you do. Are you quite sure how to spell *bête noire*—with an *e* at the end? Do you know, without hesitation, where to put the umlaut dots in *Fräulein?* (Over the *a.*)

form letters. Giant corporations will spend time and money to train their employees in writing, but send out millions of form letters in the same old bureaucratic gobbledygook.

formal. Thoreau said, "If you have any enterprise before you, try it in your old clothes." Use formal English only when you'd wear formal dress.

forms. Forms must be brief and clear, otherwise people will give the wrong answers and sign in the wrong places. When you design a form, be unmistakable. Even so, many people won't read what it says.

formula. People love formulas because they save work. Do this, do that, take three a day, repeat five times. Don't underestimate formulas; the Lord's Prayer is a formula too.

forthwith. *At once, right away.*

forwarding. Means *sending.*

fractions. Except for ½, ⅓ and ¼, fractions are *not* the simplest way of putting it. Say *one in six, four out of ten,* etc.

frequently. Say *often.*

from the point of view of. *From the point of view of pedestrians, this is dangerous = this is dangerous for pedestrians.*

function. It may *function,* but what people want to know is if it *works.*

fundamental. *Basic* means the same thing and is shorter. *Main* is still shorter.

furnish. *Give, rent, sell.*

furthermore. Another one of those long transition words. Say *and, next, then.* Or simply start your next thought.

G

gainsay. Bookish word for *deny.*

gender. Words with gender seem more personal and more alive than those without. A *poet,* an *actress,* even a *waitress* sound more interesting than an *assistant* or a *customer.*

general. Don't use the general word when you can use the specific. Don't say *tree* when you know it's an *oak;* don't say *dog* when you know it's a *schnauzer.* But don't distract the reader either by focusing on irrelevant details.

Never use the general word as an elegant-variation synonym to avoid repetition.

generations. Don't forget that times change. Your readers may belong to a generation that doesn't remember many of the things you do. Don't offhand refer to what happened twenty years ago.

genteelisms. Genteelisms are words meant to give the impression that you belong to the upper middle class. Fowler's *Modern English Usage* lists *expectorate* for *spit, odor* for *smell, perspire* for *sweat, lingerie* for *underwear,* etc. Others are *Mrs. Smith* for *my wife, pardon me* for *excuse me, I beg your pardon* for *what?, retire* for *go to bed, home* for *house.* Ironically, sociologists consider the use of genteelisms a sign that the user belongs to the *lower* middle class; as a device for status-seeking, they're therefore no good at all. Moral: It's always best to use the natural expression that comes first to mind.

gentleman. It's old-fashioned to use *gentleman* instead of *man. The gentleman behind the counter said to me = the man behind the counter said to me.*

gerund. A gerund is a verb form in *-ing* that looks like a participle but isn't. Purists insist the two forms shouldn't be used in the same way: you should say *I don't like John's swearing* instead of *I don't like John swearing.* Few people bother with the distinction.

get. Nothing wrong with *get*. A handy replacement for all kinds of formal words like *obtain, secure, develop, attain,* etc.

ghost writing. A ghost-written as-told-to article or book makes better reading than an article or book on the same subject under the ghost writer's own byline. There's nothing as readable as a story told in the first person.

gist. A good word to prod you into a summary lead. Ask yourself, "What's the gist? What's the gist?"

glad. Don't say you're glad when you're not. *I'm glad you asked that question* sounds phony to everyone.

got. Like *get,* a most useful word. Don't shy away from it.

governmentese. Before you criticize the government for its stilted, overformal language, look at the writing in your own organization. The larger it is, the more it's apt to sound like the federal government.

grammar. Grammar is useful if you apply it. Know what a verb is and express your thoughts in verbs; know what an adjective is and go easy on them. Use your knowledge of grammar to improve your writing.

46

graph. Charts and graphs are fine, but don't rely on them to tell your story. Use words to show what the graph shows. Say *The high point marks such-and-such an event in 1960; the gap between the straight line and the broken line means this-and-that.* Add the verbal to the visual.

grateful. Like *glad, grateful* is apt to sound phony. *We are grateful to you for having given us this opportunity to explain our policy*—cut it out: nobody will believe you.

gratuitous. Say *needless.*

guidance for readers. Take your readers by the hand and lead them through the text. First tell them about your plan; at each turn tell them what you're going to say next.

gymnasium. Everyone says *gym.*

H

hackneyed. Stay away from hackneyed words and phrases. But don't strain for original expressions either.

hard news. Tell the reader what he ought to know. Don't stint. Don't sacrifice important hard news for interesting, feature-type soft news. Keep an even balance.

hard sell. There's a running argument on Madison Avenue between hard sell and soft sell. Hard sell is usually tasteless but sells merchandise; soft sell is more interesting and amusing, but the client may not get his money's worth. Copywriters who have gone through the tough school of mail-order selling believe in the hard sell.

have. The perfect tense (with *have*) means the action is still going on or still has some lasting effect. *I have had lunch* means *I'm not hungry; I have heard the news* means *I know.*

have to. Handy phrase for *must, be forced to, be compelled to, be required to, be obliged to.*

haven't, hasn't, hadn't. Don't forget to use contractions.

he-or-she. English has no word meaning he-or-she. When people talk, they use *they* instead, as in *If anyone calls, tell them I'll be back in an hour.* Use the same device in writing.

he's, he'll, he'd. Again, don't forget contractions.

head. *Head* as a verb is headline jargon: SMITH TO HEAD BOARD. Avoid.

headlines. Use headlines rather than titles in your writing. Don't label a section *Profit and Loss in 1962*; say *1962 Profits Up 34%.*

hedging. Don't hedge when it's embarrassing or difficult to be straightforward. Don't hide behind vague, ponderous language. Take the bull by the horns; think of what you'd say to your reader if he sat before you—politely, truthfully, without hurting his feelings. Put down what you'd *say.*

heinous. *Ugly, wicked.*

hence. Sounds old-fashioned. Use *so.*

here's. One of the handiest contractions in the language.

herewith. Leave out. *We are sending you herewith = we are sending you.*

hereafter, hereby, heretofore. *From now on, now, until now.*

history. Everything has a history, and everything can be explained by telling it. Start at the beginning, when things were simple, and go on from there. All good popularizing tells *The story of.*

hit. A headline word. KHRUSHCHEV HITS KENNEDY doesn't mean what it says.

hitherto. *Up to now, until now.*

home. Don't use *home* when you really mean *house*. Don't say *homemaker* when you mean *housewife*.

house organ. Make it an interesting newspaper for the people in your company. Don't spoil it by pompous pronouncements from the front office.

how's. A good contraction.

how to. If your subject lends itself to how-to writing, do just that. Use the pronoun *you*, break the job down into steps, tell exactly what to do in what order. *Step 1. Do this; Step 2. Do that;* etc.

how to say no. If it's not too much of a disappointment for your reader, start right off by saying you're sorry. If you want to soften the blow, start by explaining the reasons for your refusal. Be sure to make it clear your answer is no.

how to say yes. Begin with the good news. Sometimes it's best to start with the word *yes* itself. Example: *Yes, we'll be glad to sell you the item on approval* . . . etc.

however. It's a superstition that you shouldn't start a sentence with *however*. Do it if you feel like it. If you put *however* after the first word, you're supposed to put commas before and after it; but since there's a trend toward leaving out commas, you might try to leave them out. Example: *This however turned out to be a bad idea.*

human interest. Make the most of the human interest in your material. If there are interesting sidelights, stories, anecdotes, trivial incidents, put them in. Don't neglect anything that adds to your reader's interest.

humans. Don't say *humans* when you mean *people* or *persons*.

humor. Humor is fine if it comes to you naturally. But don't strain for it. Don't drag in irrelevant funny stories. Don't use heavy humor. Above all, don't use pompous, ponderous language ironically and humorously; before you know it, it has become a habit and you're known as a humorless bore.

hyphen. Hyphens in compounds seem to be on the way out. Most such words are now written as two words without hyphen (e.g. *book club, stock option, station wagon*) or as one word (e.g. *pickup, breakdown, byproduct*). You're still supposed to use a hyphen whenever you use a compound noun as an adjective (e.g. *book-club choice*), but that rule too seems to be on the way out (e.g. *stock option deal, station wagon set*).

hypothetical case. Don't tell your readers a hypothetical case; they'll take it for granted you're thinking of a real one. (And they're often right.)

I

I. Use the pronoun *I* whenever it seems natural to do so. Don't say *the writer, the author, the undersigned*. Don't use the editorial *we* or any other kind of *we* when you mean just yourself. Don't write *we are sorry to hear of your recent illness* when it isn't your company that is sorry but just you.

I'm, I'll, I've. Use contractions whenever you can.

iceberg principle. Most magazine articles are written on the iceberg principle: nine-tenths of the material the writer has assembled stays below the surface and is never used. Use the same ratio for everything you write.

ideas. Don't go out of your way to get ideas for your writing. Deal with those that come to you from your job, your life, the natural sources of information around you.

When you wake up in the morning with a brilliant idea, it's probably no good.

identical. *Same* is shorter.

identified with. *He is identified with* = *he has a job with.*

identify. Means *recognize.*

idioms. Use idioms whenever you can. *Up-and-coming* says more than *rising.*

if. *If* is shorter than *whether* and sounds more natural in many sentences (e.g. *I don't know if he'll be there* vs. *I don't know whether he'll be there*).

When you have a choice between *if* and *when*, it's often better to use *when* (as in this sentence).

Don't use *if* for *though* as in this sentence from *Time*: *Consumer-goods companies are becoming increasingly, if belatedly, conscious of the Negro market.* When you mean *though*, say *though.*

if and when. *If* is enough.

ignorance. Always confess ignorance rather than trying to cover it up. Readers will believe what you tell them if you admit frankly that you used to be as ignorant as they, but made it your business to find out.

ill-advised. Euphemism for *stupid.* Don't use.

illustrations. Illustrate whatever you can. Pictures are best, but verbal illustrations are good too. Tell an example; give details; show how the principle applies.

image. Highly fashionable word. Avoid.

immediacy. A good public speaker will tell about "a funny thing that happened on my way here" or anyway about something that has immediacy. In the same way, a good writer uses whatever will give his subject immediate interest. Write about what happened yesterday, last week, this month.

impact. Try *shock*.

impart. *Teach, tell.*

imperative. *It is imperative = you have to.*

imperative mood. Use the imperative mood as much as you can. *Do this, use that, remember, don't forget, be sure to, keep in mind, think back, look forward to, note, compare, file and forget.*

impersonal. Impersonal writing is stiffer, harder to read, longer. Instead of *it is suggested that care should be taken* say *please take care.*

impetus. Try *drive, push*.

implement. The verb *to implement* is a famous Washington gobbledygook word. To *implement a policy* means to *carry it out*.

imply. *This implies = this means.*

impulse. Again, try *drive* or *push*.

in other words. Unnecessary connective. Leave out; try a colon.

inaccurate. Euphemism meaning *wrong*. You might as well say *wrong*.

inadvertency. It happened by mistake.

inasmuch as. A favorite with bureaucrats. Say *since*.

inaugurate. *Start.*

incentive. *Drive, push.*

inception. Also means *start* or *beginning*.

incident. What happened.

inclement weather. Rain or snow.

inconsiderable. *Slight, small, little.*

inconvenient. A bother.

increase. *Rise, grow, go up.*

indeed. A formal word. In speaking, people often raise their voice instead: *I am indeed happy to see you = I am happy to see you.*

indefinite. *Vague, unnamed.*

indention. Indention is used to mark a new paragraph and give the reader a slight break. Use indention freely. Newspaper copyreaders paragraph more often and more casually than other writers. Follow their example.

indicate. Usually means *show*; sometimes *hint.*

indirect questions. Turn indirect questions into direct questions whenever you can. Instead of *There was a long discussion whether this was a question of law or of fact* write *There was a long discussion: was this a question of law or of fact?*

individual. Don't use the five-syllable word *individual* when you mean *person.* Don't use it either when you mean *for one,* as in *individual portions.*

indulge in. Old-fashioned. Rewrite. Try *eat, drink, use.*

infer. Often confused with *imply.* Means *think* or *figure.*

inferior. Means *poor.*

infinite. *Endless.*

infinitive. The active voice of the verb is better. Instead of *He planned to organize an association* try *He thought he'd organize an association.*

inform. *Tell* is shorter.

informal. Informal English is right for all occasions except official speeches, court decisions, etc. Use informal English whenever you'd talk informally to your reader.

initial. Means *first.*

initials. It's handy to use initials for short. Follow newspaper pratice and say JFK, etc.

initiate. *Start.*

innuendo. *Hint.*

inquire. Say *ask.*

inquiry. Say *question.* When you write a letter of inquiry, put in a question with a question mark.

insert, insertion. *Put in.*

insight. Pet word of mystics and *gestalt* psychologists. Avoid.

insignificant. Means *slight.*

instance. *In this instance = here.*

institute. *Start, set up.*

institutional ads. They're pompous by definition—good examples of how not to write.

instructions. Use the step-by-step cookbook method. Stick to the *you* style. Remember all those cartoons about instructions how to assemble Christmas toys.

instrumental. *He was instrumental = he helped.*

insults. Don't insult your reader, directly or indirectly. Don't write *you must realize, you agreed, you must have been aware, it is well known,* etc.

insure. Don't say *insure* when you mean *make sure.*

intelligence of readers. Don't underrate your readers' intelligence. Never talk down to them. Take it for granted they're at least as smart as you are.

intentional. *Meant.*

intermission. Means *break.*

international. It's a good rule of thumb to use as many "international" words as possible—names, numbers, place names, dates, words meaning things used everywhere, e.g. *food, water, milk, gasoline, automobile, movies.* Readers can't misunderstand words like that.

interpose. Say *put in, cut in.*

interregnum. *Break, gap.*

interrogate. Say *ask, question.*

interval. Say *gap.*

interview. The modern interview was invented in 1836 by James Gordon Bennett. There's no better way to make things readable. Ask someone who knows and get his answers down verbatim.

Try to make your quotes from printed sources sound like an interview. *"We are still looking for an answer," says Dr. Frank W. Morton. "The problem is . . ."*

intimate. *Close.*

into. You can often shorten it to *in.*

introduction. Most introductions are unnecessary. Get to the point immediately. It's a useful rule of thumb to cut the first three paragraphs and start with paragraph 4.

inundate. Say *flood.*

inure to. *It inures to the benefit of = it benefits.*

inversion. Inversion is always unnatural. Some examples from *Time: Appraised she . . . confessed he . . . snorted he. . . .* Don't copy.

inverted pyramid. Newspaper term for the usual upside-down structure of a story: first the outcome, climax, final result; then more details, some background; next, still more details, more background; etc. Use the inverted pyramid for letters, reports, memos, other factual writing. Start by spilling the beans; then, by stages, go back to the beginning.

investigate. Try *study, look into.*

involve. The shortest synonym is *mean. Let me explain what is involved = let me explain what this means.*

involved. Usually unnecessary. *Some of the employees involved complained = some employees complained.*

-ion. Words ending in *-ion* are the most common abstract, formal words. Go through your writing and try to weed out all the *-ion* words. It does wonders for your style.

irony. Don't use irony: your reader may not feel exactly the same way about things. Or your irony may go past him.

irrelevant. *Pointless.*

is. Watch *is, are, was* and *were* in your writing. They're signs that you use too many nouns instead of verbs. Change your predicates to verbs. Get rid of *is.*

isn't. Remember contractions.

issue. Say *put out.*

it. *It* can often be left out at the beginning of a sentence. *Looks like rain. Seems we're in for trouble.*

Don't use *it* in referring to an organization people think of as *they.* Write *We passed this on to our branch office; they'll get in touch with you.*

it goes without saying. Then don't say it.

it's, it'll. More contractions to remember.

it's me. Never mind the old argument. No one says *It is I.*

italics. Underline for emphasis; use italics in print. Don't throw away the only device for showing stress in writing.

-ize. Go easy on *-ize* words. Don't *finalize, utilize, conceptualize, personalize,* etc.

J

jargon. Jargon means the language of a special field, like sports jargon, business jargon. Write so that no one can tell from your style what subject you're dealing with.

jeopardize. Say *risk*.

juncture. *At this juncture = at this time, now.*

juvenile. Don't use the long word *juvenile* whenever you talk of children and teenagers.

K

key element. Before you start writing, focus on the key element of your material. Once you've found it, use it for the lead; the rest will follow naturally.

kind of, sort of. Good idiomatic adverbs. Use them.

kindly. Don't use *kindly* as a synonym for *please*. Say *please*.

know. "I know but I can't explain." Then you don't know.

L

l. Use simple spelling. Use one *l* in *traveling, canceling, totaling, jeweler,* etc.

laboratory. Say *lab*.

lack. Rewrite. *Due to their lack of funds = since they had no money.*

lad. Bookish. Say *boy, young man*.

lady. Don't say *lady* when you mean *woman*. Sounds genteel.

Lao-tse. Lao-tse, the founder of Taoism, never wrote a line until he was an old man. On his trip to retirement in the mountains, he was held up by a frontier guard who insisted he should put his doctrine in writing. So he wrote the *Tao-te-king* in 5,000 words—the shortest scripture known to man. Let that be a lesson to you.

last line. It's usually a good idea to cut the last line.

Latin. Don't use Latin words. Say it in English.

lead. Don't start with an introduction; start with a news-paper-type lead. Write a first sentence that could be boiled down into a headline.

legwork. The more facts you've got, the better you'll write.

legal writing. Lawyers are used to writing so that nobody can possibly misunderstand; they also like to use terms whose meaning has been decided by the courts. The result is a language of their own where every reference is spelled out again and again and the same phrases are used over and over. Most of this language is unnecessary even in legal documents; elsewhere it's annoying and silly. Write so that ordinary people will understand what you mean.

lengthy. Say *long*.

less vs. fewer. An old argument among grammarians. Don't worry about it.

58

lest. Bookish. *Put on your rubbers lest you catch cold.* Nobody talks like that: say *or.*

let's. Don't overdo the business of talking about yourself and your readers as *we* and *us.* It's better to say *you. Let's suppose = suppose.*

let's call him. Be frank about fictitious names. Say *let's call him Jenkins.*

let's say. Good casual way of introducing an example.

letters. Letters (*a, b, c*) are good for listing but numbers are better. By the time you get to *h,* it's easier for the reader if you say 8.

And don't use letters instead of fictitious names.

level. Overused. *For people at the middle-income level = for middle-income people.*

library. Learn how to use a library for better writing. With all the facts and figures within easy reach, there's no excuse for vague, pompous, unspecific writing. Find what you need to know, take notes, and fill your writing with good, readable substance.

lieu. *In lieu of = instead of.*

like. Use *like* as a conjunction if that's the natural way you talk. But don't go out of your way to use folksy grammar like some advertisers do.

likewise. Heavy connective. Change it to *too.*

limit, limitation. Try *check, ceiling, top, floor.*

Lincoln's Doctor's Dog. In the 30s someone thought up this surefire title for a bestseller. (What are the most popular books about? Lincoln, doctors, and dogs.) Still a good reminder of what people are most interested in—celebrities, health and objects of affection.

line. Don't say *line* when you mean *field* or *job*.

list. It's handy to give readers an itemized list. But keep each item separate; don't start with a half-sentence and give the reader a list of second halves. Don't do it this way:

Each item on your list must be:
1. *self-contained.*
2. *one sentence only. Don't add a second sentence.*
3. *different from the rest.*

This way is better:

Here's how to make a list:
1. *Use only self-contained items.*
2. *Make each item different from the rest.*
3. *Use only one sentence per item.*

literally. Avoid. You probably mean just the opposite.

literary criticism. Don't be pompous. Don't pretend you know more about a book than the author.

literature. Don't try to follow literary models or develop a literary style. Don't try to produce literature when you're supposed to do a job.

little. Cut out the words *a little*; it usually helps.

loan. Grammarians argue whether you should use *loan* as a verb. Most people do.

locality. Say *town, village*—whatever it is.

locate. Usually means *find*.

logic. Logic is a fine thing for setting up computer programs, but the human mind doesn't always work that way. Remember that.

loose sentences. Use loose sentences rather than periodic sentences (where you have to wait until the end for the main clause). Instead of *Jittery about the political situation, the stock market was sluggish,* say *The stock market was sluggish*

60

because it was jittery about the political situation. Loose sentences are easier to read.

M

magazines. Literary magazines and journals of opinion are dying out; news magazines and digests are growing. What most readers want are facts, told in brief.

magnitude. Say *size*.

mail order. Mail-order advertising can be tested to see if it works; if no orders come in, it's no good. Tests prove that copy has to be specific and tell in detail what the customer will get for his money.

main point. Start with the main point. Tell the gist. Spill the beans.

major. Try *big, large.*

majority. *The majority of = most.*

make the acquaintance of. *Meet, get to know.*

maladjusted. Common euphemism for *neurotic.*

mandatory. *Must, has to be.*

manage. A good word, but *run* is even shorter.

manuals. Write any instruction manual in cookbook style. Break the job down into small steps and list the steps. 1. *Do this;* 2. *Do that;* 3. *Do that;* etc.

Think of various problems that may come up, special cases, emergencies, the unusual. Try to foresee the questions the manual will have to answer on the job.

map. Headline word for *plan,* e.g. FBI MAPS DRIVE. Avoid.

materialize. Work out, show up.

materially. How about *much?*

mathematics. Wouldn't *math* do?

matter of fact. As *a matter of fact* is often used as an empty phrase. Cut it out; you'll probably find you didn't need it.

maximum. Try *most, top, highest, best.*

may. It's usually more idiomatic to say *can.*

me. Say *it's me* and *between you and me.*

medical writing. Medical writing is a mixture of terse, straightforward case histories and ponderous discussion of theory. If you're a doctor, try to keep everything as sharp and clear as your case histories.

memos. Memos are supposed to be brief reminders. Jot down what you'd say to the guy or what you did say to him—in the same words. In a memo, anything goes. *Joe: OK by me* is a good style model for a memo.

Corporations often pay attention to letter writing because they know the public relations value of better letters. Nobody does anything about better memos. Too bad.

mention. It's shorter to write *say* or *name.*

metaphors. Metaphors are words used for something different from what they meant originally. (*Corporation* comes from *corpus,* body; a *president* is someone who sits at the head of the table.) Go slow in using fresh metaphors of your own; your reader may not be as familiar with golf or football as you are.

minimize. Often used for *underrate.*

Mr. Smith. Don't say *Mr. Smith* (or whatever) when you mean your husband. Say *my husband*.

Mrs. Smith. Ditto. Say *my wife*.

mirror. Chuang-tse, the Chinese sage, said, "A wise man uses his mind like a mirror; it stays passive and gives back what it receives without concealment." Don't editorialize; just give the facts.

modifier. Adjectives modify nouns, adverbs modify verbs. Use as few modifiers as possible; tell your story in verbs and nouns.

moral. There's a moral at the end of each of Aesop's fables. Tell the meaning of your story; show the point you want to make.

morale. Fashionable word. Rewrite. *High morale = people feel good.*

moreover. Ponderous connective. Use *then.* Or rewrite so that no transition word is needed.

motivate, motivation. Try *lead, push, drive.*

much obliged. Means *thank you.*

"Murder your darlings." Sir Arthur Quiller-Couch said, "Whenever you feel an impulse to perpetrate a piece of exceptionally fine writing, obey it—wholeheartedly—and delete it before sending your manuscript to press. *Murder your darlings.*"

He's right. Strike out whatever you're specially proud of. Be ruthless.

mustn't. Handy contraction.

myself. Don't use *myself* when you mean *I* or *me.*

N

name dropping. Name dropping in print is just as bad as in conversation. Don't show off by quoting every book you've ever read. Albert Schweitzer said this, C. G. Jung said that, T. S. Eliot said the other. So what? Would you quote it to your reader even if you didn't give the source?

names. Nothing is more readable than names. Use names—don't say A, B and C, don't write about the employee, the testator, the plaintiff, the assistant, the supervisor, the clerk, the teacher, the recipient. Give their names or invent names for them. Give them first names, nicknames, the kind of names people use.

You don't like to be addressed as *occupant*, do you?

narrate. *He narrated the incident* = *he told what happened.*

nature. Empty all-purpose word. *It was something in the nature of an event* = *it was an event.*

nay. Sounds bookish. Avoid.

near. *In the near future* = *soon.*

necessitate. Rewrite. *My transfer to California necessitated the removal of all my furniture* = *when I was shifted to California I had to move all my furniture.*

necessity. *Need* will usually do.

needless to say. Then don't say it.

negate. Try *deny, cancel, wipe out.*

negative words. Don't use words with negative meanings; say the same thing with *no* or *not.* Instead of *failure* say *he didn't;* instead of *he was absent, he wasn't there;* instead of *lack of food, no food.*

negligible. *Small, little.*

neighborhood. *In the neighborhood of = about, around.*

nevertheless. Another one of the heavy connectives. Rewrite and leave out; or use *but.*

new words. Don't coin new words; don't write blithely of *uncomfortability, non-homeownership, multi-traditionalism.*

news magazines. Study news magazines and learn how they shorten and digest the news. Don't copy their special tricks and quirks; but learn from them how to shorten sentences, leave out unnecessary words, use punctuation for brevity.

newsletters. Learn from newsletters too. Adapt their style for your own reports and letters.

newspapers. Learn from newspapers. Study the language of headlines, but don't fall into headline jargon. Study the inverted pyramid method of news reports. (See also **inverted pyramid.**) Watch how they use short paragraphs, subheads, quotes.

nicknames. Use nicknames in writing when you'd use nicknames in speaking. When someone is universally called Joe, there isn't much point in calling him Joseph.

no. *No* is a handy word. Use it in such simple sentences as *the court said no* (without quotation marks) and in such phrases as *it was no good* or *it was no use.*

nominal. Means *small.*

non-. Words with *non-* are usually bookish; avoid them. The trend is to leave out the hyphen, as in *nonfiction, nonentity.*

none. Strict grammarians say you must say *none is.* Most people though say *none are.*

not. *Not* is usually contracted to *n't* in speaking; do it often in writing. When you want to stress it, underline it: an under-lined *not* can't be overlooked.

not un-. Beware of cumbersome *not un-* phrases. Don't say *not unaware of, not unreasonable,* etc. Cross out *not un-* and say *aware of, reasonable.*

not writing. Talk is better and simpler than writing. Do you have to write this down? Would a phone call do? Could you walk down the hall instead of writing a memo? Always remember that writing is a substitute for talking. Sometimes the best way to be brief is not to write at all.

note-taking. When you take notes, look for simple, read-able items. Prepare for your digressions, anecdotes and illus-trations. Don't neglect the trivial; be on the lookout for it.

notes. Make your reference notes and footnotes as light and inconspicuous as you can. Give just what is needed for reference and nothing more. But don't put your notes in smaller type size. Readers will have to use the same eyes for the notes as for the text: don't punish them with 6-point type.

notwithstanding. Much too long. Say *in spite of, even though*.

noun. Don't use a noun when you can use a verb. Don't fill your writing, as Fowler says, with "a compost of nouny abstractions."

noun adjectives. Headline writers and news magazine edi-tors love noun adjectives because they're brief. It takes less space to say *a Kremlin spokesman* than *a spokesman of the Kremlin.* But don't use a noun adjective instead of a real adjective; don't say *Brazil president* instead of *president of Brazil* (it should be *Brazilian president*).

Noun adjectives are handy but should be used with care.

noun adjectives (*Contd.*)

They're a newspaper device and don't come naturally to people in conversation.

numbers. Give numbers (in Arabic numerals) whenever you can. They're clear, brief and specific. There's no better way to make the reader understand what you're talking about.

numerous. Say *many*.

O

obits. Obits in the paper are often models of good writing. They always start with a classic summary lead and tell in a nutshell who the person was and what he did. If you want to learn how to be brief, read obits.

objective. *Aim.*

obligate, obligatory. *Bind, binding.*

obliged. Usually means *grateful, thank you.*

observe. Try *notice, see, keep.*

observance. Rewrite with *keep, follow.* Or leave out.

obtain. Means *get.*

obvious. Say *plain* or *clear.* Be careful not to insult your reader.

occasion. Empty word; leave out. *This occasion reminds me of = this reminds me of.*

occupation. Say *job, work, business.*

occur. Say *happen.*

odor. Genteelism for *smell.*

of course. Often used patronizingly, in the sense of *everybody knows that.* Don't tell the reader he's stupid.

of whether. Say *whether. The question of whether = the question whether.*

omission. What was left out.

omit. *Cut, leave out.*

on or about. Legal phrase, as in *this year we'll celebrate Christmas on or about December 25* (as a lawyer might say).

on the basis of. Try *by* or *under.*

one. The indefinite pronoun often sounds stuffy. When you mean *I,* say *I. It reminds one of = it reminds me of.*

one-syllable words. One-syllable words are fine, but it's not the number of syllables that matters but the simplicity or complexity of the words. Some one-syllable words are hard to understand, like *pi, kith, trope.* But most are better than longer words.

operate. Try *run.*

opine. Worn-out humor. Say *think, say.*

opinion. Don't inject your own opinions into what you're writing. Did anybody ask you? If not, keep your opinions to yourself.

opportune. *Proper, handy.*

opportunity. *Chance* is shorter. And don't answer complaints with *we thank you for giving us the opportunity to explain.* Sounds phony.

optimism. Say *hope.*

optimistic. Say *hopeful, cheerful.*

order. *In order to = to.*

organizaton. If it's a company, call it a *company.* If it's your company, say *we.*

originality. Don't try for originality: "No one can be original by trying," said Somerset Maugham. If you *are* original, people will notice anyway.

originate. Means *start, come from.*
ostensibly. *On the face of it.*
other than. Legalistic, bookish phrase. Say *except.*
oust. Headline jargon for *fire, drive out, throw out.*
outline. Overused. Say *give, tell, list, sketch, explain.*
outlines. Courses and textbooks in composition always insist you must make an outline. Their recipe for writing is, Draw up a detailed list of your topics and subtopics with the proper numerals, letters and indentions; then write by filling in the places on your outline with enough substance to make nice, neat paragraphs.

If you want to be brief, the outline method of writing is no good. It tempts you to treat everything at equal length and in equal depth; it forces your thoughts into a prearranged shape.

Learn to write without an outline. Settle beforehand on a lead, a conclusion, and the rough order of what to say in between. Then sit down with your assembled notes and write. Let your report, letter, memo, article take its own shape. Talk freely to your reader.

overall. Fashionable word meaning *whole.*

P

pact. Headline word for *contract, treaty, agreement.* Avoid.
parables. The best method for teaching religious and ethical principles. Study Jesus' parables as examples of good writing and teaching.

69

paradox. A paradox is a truth, strikingly phrased so that people will say, "It *can't* be true!" There's nothing more memorable or effective. *Blessed are the meek* is a paradox; so is $e = mc^2$.

It is also a paradox that it takes time to be brief.

paragraph. A paragraph is simply a longer break between sentences, marked by starting a new line. Don't lose any sleep over paragraph structure or paragraph unity. When more than a period is called for, start a new paragraph; that's all. Keep your paragraphs short; follow newspaper practice.

parataxis. Parataxis means writing without connecting conjunctions or pronouns, e.g. *I tried; I couldn't do it. He says it's useless. I know a fellow used to live here.* Parataxis is one of the secrets of brevity.

pardon me. Genteelism for *excuse me* or *what?*

parentheses. Use parentheses freely to throw things in casually. (Parentheses mean "You can skip this.")

parlay. Bookish word for using a small stake to make a fortune. Don't use.

participate. *Take part, be one of, go along.*

particularly. Try *too, well, much.*

parts of speech. There's a rank order among the parts of speech. Prefer verbs to nouns, nouns to adjectives and adverbs. Always put your thoughts in the strongest form.

party. Don't use *party* for *person.*

patently. *Plainly, clearly.*

paucity. Rewrite. Say *few* or *little.*

pause. A good speaker knows how to use a pause for effect. Do the same in writing. Use dashes and paragraphs freely.

pecuniary. Say *money. Pecuniary difficulties = money troubles.*

peer. Educational and sociological jargon. *Peer groups* in education means children of the same age. Avoid.

pending. Say *until.*

people. Put people in your writing; there's nothing more interesting to readers. Use the word *people* itself often, e.g. *I talked to the Universal Gadgets people and they told me . . .*

per annum. A *year.*

per diem. A *day.*

per se. Leave out. Usually means nothing.

perceive. *See, make out.*

percentage. Percentages are better than vague words like *most, few,* etc. Phrases like *one in eight* or *two out of three* are still better.

perfect tense. Use the perfect tense for something that's still going on or has a lasting effect. In February write *we have had a very cold winter;* in July write *we had a very cold winter.*

perfectly. Strike out; if you need an adverb, try *quite.*

period. It's good to use many periods because that's a sign your sentences are short. But be on the lookout for breaks where you can replace periods with colons or semicolons. This will tie together closely related sentences and make for faster reading. When you put a semicolon or colon instead of a period, change the capital to lower case.

period of. Leave out. *For a period of twenty years = for twenty years.*

periodic sentences. Stay away from periodic sentences like *Considering the lateness of the hour and the exhausting day I've had, and in view of the fact that I'll have to get up very early tomorrow morning, I think I'll go to bed.* Don't build up to what you're going to say. Say it.

permission. *I got permission = they let me.*

71

permit. *Let, leave.*

pernicious. *Bad, harmful.*

personal letters. Women are usually better letter writers than men. Personal letters should be newsy and warm. So, for that matter, should business letters.

personal sentences. Questions (*why not?*), commands (*don't forget!*), elliptical answers (*he wasn't*), and quoted spoken sentences have a personal feeling that straight declarative sentences have not. Use as many personal sentences as you can. In the average newspaper or magazine article, one in seven sentences is personal.

personal words. Names, personal pronouns and other words meaning people make your writing interesting and easy to read. In a typical newspaper or magazine article, the average sentence has at least one personal word in it; usually it's the subject. Avoid impersonal writing. Tell what people do or did.

personnel. Say *staff, employees.*

perspire. *Sweat.*

pertain. Go *with, have to do with, belong to.*

pertinent. *To the point.*

peruse. *Read.*

phenomenon. Long word, usually better left out. *This phenomenon was highly unusual = this was highly unusual.*

philosophy. Don't use when you mean *thinking. His philosophy of merchandising was = he thought merchandising should be.*

phony. Be sure your writing doesn't sound phony; readers will see through it at once. Say what you mean; don't try to cover up. What would *you* think of this if someone else had written it? Remember readers are just as smart as you are.

72

pictures. Pictures are fine, but it's up to you to explain them and tie them to your text. The famous Chinese proverb that a picture is worth 10,000 words is a myth. Show people what to see.

place. Don't use *place* for *put*. Sounds genteel.

plain style. There are two great styles in literature—plain and ornate. Take pride in your plain style; write like Defoe, Swift, Benjamin Franklin, Mark Twain.

platitude. A platitude is something everybody knows. Have you written a sentence like "Nobody knows what's going to happen next year?" Cross it out.

please. A good word to use in writing. Makes the reader feel good. Say *please* often—please.

plethora. Bookish word. Means *too much, an awful lot.*

plot. If you can, tell your story with some sort of plot. Talk about the court case, the piece of research, the current event, as if you were telling a good, suspenseful short story. Make the reader ask what happened next.

plural. Use plurals to save articles. *Taxpayers* is shorter than *a taxpayer* or *the taxpayer.*

point of view. Overused. *From the point of view of the housewife = for the housewife.*

policy. Often used for brushoffs: *It has been for many years our company policy = no.* Avoid.

polite no. Say thank you for the offer or suggestion and explain frankly the reasons why you can't accept it. Courtesy is fine, but don't try to make your no sound like yes.

polity. Don't use that word. Most readers will think it's a misprint for *policy.*

polysyllabic humor. It isn't funny to write about *succulent bivalves* or *postprandial levity.* Cut it out. There's always a danger that you'll fall into the habit and use such phrases regularly.

pomposity. Everybody who writes is apt to sound pompous from time to time. Fight pomposity at every step. Take off your coat and tie—mentally and physically. Tell it to Joe. Don't take yourself seriously for a moment.

popular. Don't be afraid of popular style. Shakespeare wrote for the crowd; Dickens published his novels as shilling serials.

popularization. The secret of popularization is to tell the human story. Don't write about problems and issues; write about people. Give the reader someone to identify himself with.

portion. Make it *part*.

position. Don't use when you mean *job*. *We are now in a position to tell you* = *we can tell you now*.

positively. Say *quite*; or leave out.

possessive case. Headline and news magazine writers have gone back to the possessive *'s* for things as well as for people. *At week's end, the book's appeal, the company's progress*. In ordinary talk, people use *of*: they say *at the end of the week, the appeal of the book, the progress of the company*. The possessive *'s* is shorter, but use it only when it sounds natural to you.

possibility. Say *chance*.

postpone. Say *put off, hold up*.

postulate. Use *say, claim*.

posture. Fashionable word for a *stand* or *view*. Avoid.

potential. Try *maybe, could be*.

practically. Long word for *almost, nearly*.

precede. Go or *come before*.

74

precision. Thorstein Veblen said, "It is contended that a punctilious use of ancient and accredited locutions will serve to convey thought more adequately and more precisely than would the straightforward use of the latest form of spoken English; whereas it is notorious that the ideas of today are effectively expressed in the slang of today."

predicament. Long word for *trouble* or *fix*.

predicate. Make your predicate a verb; when you have used a noun with *is, was, are* or *were*, try rewriting the sentence, using an active verb.

predominantly. *Chiefly, mainly, mostly.*

prefixes. Cut down on words with prefixes; replace words beginning with *ad-, con-, de-, dis-, ex-, in-, inter-, re-, non-, un-, pre-, pro-, trans-*, etc.

prejudice. *Bias* is shorter.

preliminary to. *Before.*

premises. You mean *building* or *house*.

preparatory to. *Before.*

prepare. Often used for *make, fix*.

preponderantly. *Mainly, chiefly, mostly.*

prepositions. Use simple, one-syllable prepositions whenever you can. Avoid compounds like *in accordance with, with reference to, for the purpose of, in order to, notwithstanding the fact that*.

presage. The common word is *predict*.

present. At *present* means *now*. Don't use *at present* for polite brushoffs.

present tense. Use the present tense instead of the past tense whenever you can—makes it sound livelier. Try your hand with this when you quote people or state their views. Write *he says, he is for, he criticizes, he agrees*, etc.

presently. Although *presently* used to mean *soon,* most people today use it when they mean *now.* Avoid it; say *now.*

preserve. Say *keep.*

press release. Try to forget you're interested. Write it so you *would* be interested if you were a casual reader.

presume. *Dr. Livingstone, I presume?* Say *think.*

pretty. Usually unnecessary as an adverb. Cross it out.

prevail upon. *Urge, push, put up to.*

prevalent. *Common.*

previous. Say *earlier.*

primarily. Say *chiefly, mainly, mostly.*

primary. *First, main. The primary purpose = the main purpose.*

prime. Bookish word. Say *best.*

principally. Again means *mainly, chiefly, mostly.*

prior to. Say *before.*

probe. Headline word for *study, look into, test, quiz, check.*

procedure. How to do it; the way it's done.

proceed. *Go on, go ahead.*

procure. Say *get.*

productive of. Rewrite. Say *yield.*

proficient. *Good at, skilled.*

profound. *Deep.*

progressive tenses. Progressive tenses (*I am writing, I was sleeping, I'll be waiting*) are verb forms that show that an action is in progress. Use the progressive tense whenever you have a choice. *We'll be writing you soon* means a little more than *we'll write you soon;* it carries the sense of somebody at work writing a letter.

project. Fancy word for *job* or *plan.*

pronouncement. What was said.

pronouns. Use pronouns instead of repeating the noun: that's what pronouns are for. Don't use elegant variation. Write *the king . . . he . . . he;* don't write *the king . . . the monarch . . . the ruler . . . the royal visitor.* And don't repeat the noun endlessly either, legal style: *the plaintiff . . . the plaintiff . . . the plaintiff . . . the plaintiff.* There's nothing wrong with repeating *he.* Use pronouns.

pronunciation. Don't use words that give people difficulty in pronunciation, e.g. *chimera* (kyeMEEra), *grimace* (gri-MAYCE), *congeries* (conJEERees), *vagary* (vaGARey), *schism* (SIZm), *heinous* (HAYnous). When people aren't sure how to pronounce a word, they don't use it, and when they don't use it, they're apt to be unfamiliar with its meaning. Watch out for such words and avoid them.

proper names. Use proper names—real or fictitious. Names make news; they also make any kind of writing more interesting to read.

proportion. Don't use when you mean *size* or *amount.*

proposition. Empty word. *I refuse to take this proposition seriously* = *I refuse to take this seriously.*

proverbs. Proverbs are distilled experience, phrased to be memorable. They're models of brevity. Learn from proverbs how to say much in little.

provide. *The law provides* = *the law says* or *calls for.*

provided, providing that. Say *if.*

psychoanalysis. Psychoanalysis treats neurotics by letting them talk on and on and on. Next time you overwhelm your reader with a flood of words, think whether you're not really doing it because it makes you feel good. Say only what's necessary for the job in hand.

punctuation. Use punctuation to speed up reading. Leave

out commas whenever possible and change periods to semi-colons and colons between closely related sentences. On the other hand, give the reader more paragraph breaks.

purchase. Say *buy.*

purport. Try *claim, mean.*

purpose. *For the purpose of* = *for.*

pursuant to. Compound preposition with a legal flavor. Say *by* or *under.*

pursue. Means *follow, chase, go after, run after.*

purview. Try *reach, scope.*

puzzles. Everybody is interested in a mystery or puzzle. If you can tell your story in the form of a puzzle, by all means do so. Raise a question in the reader's mind, build up suspense, then come up with the solution.

Q

Q and A. Questions and answers are fine for writing, but be sure they sound like the real thing. Use a tape recorder or else write as if you'd used one. Don't just slice your material into equal sections and preface each with a question. Sounds deadly.

qua. Latin for *as.* Say *as.*

qualifications. Lawyers hate to make a statement without qualifications. When they've written *all male citizens between 21 and 65,* they feel nervous and change it to *all male citizens between 21 and 65, other than those who have been convicted*

qualifications (*Contd.*)

of a felony; then they look at it again and make it *all male citizens between 21 and 65 other than those who have been convicted of a felony unless the sentence has been reversed.* The right way to do it is to make a statement and talk about qualifications later.

Write like a professional writer, not like a lawyer. Don't spoil everything you say by needless qualifications.

qualified. Say *able, fit.*

qualities. Don't write about the qualities of things or people. Tell what they do or did.

questionnaires. When you draw up a questionnaire, ask about things and facts, not about people's feelings, attitudes and preferences. Don't invite them to lie, exaggerate, pretend.

questions. Ask questions. Ask the reader questions, ask yourself questions, quote questions asked by others. One of the most readable marks on paper is a question mark. Create suspense by raising questions and make your readers eager to know the answers.

quotation marks. Use quotation marks only for quotes. Don't use them for emphasis; the right device for emphasis is underlining (italics in print). And don't use quotation marks to set off colloquial expressions. When you use them, use them as part of your own language; don't pretend you're quoting someone else. Don't write *this is something to "write home about."* Write *this is something to write home about* (without quotation marks). Or, if you're really ashamed of the phrase, say something else.

Don't use quotation marks in sentences like *he said yes* or *they asked why.*

American publishers use double quotation marks for ordinary quotes and single quotation marks for quotes within

79

quotes. British publishers do it the other way round. Seems simpler and easier on the eyes.

quotes. Use quotes freely to make your writing more interesting. Quote what people said rather than what they wrote. Use their exact words; it sounds better.

Use simple speech tags like *said, answered* or *added.* Don't dress them up with adverbs like *he said belligerently* or *she answered obligingly.* Don't use verbs like *he frowned* or *she shrugged.*

Put the speech tag where it fits naturally. Don't write "*I am ready,*" *he said,* "*to go.*" Write "*I am ready to go,*" *he said.*

R

range. Give readers a quick idea of statistical figures by showing the range. Say *prices from $3.98 to $25,000,* etc.

rapid reading. Speed reading courses teach the art of skimming and bypassing everything that's unessential. Learn to write so that speed reading is unnecessary. Make every word count. Give the reader everything he needs to know and not a word more.

rather. Affected word trying to make it sound casual. Leave out. Instead of *I found it rather pleasant to watch* say *I found it pleasant to watch.*

rationale. Fashionable long word for *reason.*

re. Short, but not English. Usually it's better to rewrite.

80

*Re the offer from Hollywood, I advise you to turn it down =
I advise you to turn down the offer from Hollywood.*

readability. Readable means interesting and easy to read.
Don't sacrifice readability for brevity. If you cut out a necessary
explanation or illustration, you'll save space but it may take
your reader more time and effort to read and understand
what's left. Don't try to save space and paper; save actual
reading time. Readability may call for more words, but they'll
be read more quickly.

reader's side. Always remember the reader's side. Think
of how he feels. He doesn't want to be taught; he doesn't want
to be sold; he doesn't want to be convinced. He has probably
other things on his mind; he's probably not interested in what
you have to say. How would *you* feel if you were in his place?

reader's questions. Be sure to answer questions in the
reader's mind. It's your business to foresee them and answer
them. Beware of loose ends.

reading for writing. Don't just echo what you've read.
Don't copy your sources of information; digest what they said
and write what *you* would say to your reader if he sat before
you. Quote only what's worth quoting in the original words.

In general, read what will help lighten your style. Read
fiction, newspaper features and columns, popular magazines.
Too much heavy reading will poison your style.

Don't read too many books. William Hazlitt said, "Books
serve as a screen to keep us from a knowledge of things."

real subject. Ask yourself, What is the real subject? Why
am I writing this? What am I trying to do? Often, without
thinking about it, you play an elaborate game of let's pretend.
You try to sell something and pretend you're making a survey;
you answer a complaint and pretend you give information; you

try to get someone to do something and pretend you're simply reporting. Don't tie yourself up in knots trying to play your little game by your self-imposed rules. Drop the mask; say what's on your mind; deal with your real subject. Most of your writing problems will then solve themselves.

realism. Add a touch of realism whenever you can. Give people's ages, income, addresses. Mention how they're dressed, how their voices sound. If they're angry, stubborn, embarrassed, mention that too.

realize. *Understand, know.* Don't say *I am sure you realize:* sounds patronizing and insulting.

reason. Overused to show cause and effect. It's simpler to say *since* or *because* or use a colon. *The reason for my delay was that I missed the bus = I was late because I missed the bus. Many people don't vote for the simple reason that they are too lazy = many people don't vote: they're too lazy.*

Most people say *the reason is because*; grammarians insist it should be *the reason is that.* The best thing is to rewrite the sentence and leave out *the reason is.*

Reason: A handy device, used often by *Time.*

receive. Say *get.*

recently. Sounds formal. Say *just, last week, last month,* etc.

reduce. *Cut, cut down, take off.*

redundancy. Information theory says that redundancy (repetition) is necessary to make sure a message will get through. If you say things over and over, people are bound to hear and remember it. If you're too brief and cut out all repetitions, you may wind up being cryptic. Don't be so brief as to baffle your reader. Keep some redundancy.

reference. *In reference to, with reference to:* say *on, about,* or rewrite. *With reference to the forthcoming holidays, we*

reference (*Contd.*)

have made the following arrangements = we've made these arrangements for the holidays.

reflect. Often used for *show. The balance sheet reflects last year's profits = the balance sheet shows last year's profits.*

refrain. Rewrite. *He refrained from = he didn't, he wasn't,* etc.

refusals. Be straightforward. Start with politely saying no. If you're afraid the reader will be hurt or disappointed, build up to your *no* by explaining why. Don't pussyfoot; don't mumble your *no* so it almost sounds like *yes.*

regard. *In regard to, with regard to.* Say *on, about,* or rewrite. *In regard to your inquiry, I am sending you our booklet = I am sending you our booklet.*

regret. Say *I am sorry, we're sorry* rather than *we regret.* Sounds more as if you meant it.

regularly. *As a rule.*

regulation. *Rule* is shorter.

reiterate. You mean *repeat.*

reject. *Turn down, say no.*

relate. *Tell.*

relative pronouns. Don't use the heavy relative pronoun *which* if you can help it; change it to *that* or leave it out. *The law which was passed last year = the law that was passed last year. The show which I saw last night = the show I saw last night.*

It is often better to change *which* clauses into independent sentences. *The President held a press conference yesterday in which he dealt at length with the situation in South East Asia = The President held a press conference yesterday. He dealt at length with the situation in South East Asia.* (See also **that** and **which.**)

relative to. Try *on*, *about*, *of*, *for*.

reluctant. *Unwilling*.

remark. Use *say*. *His remark* = *what he said*.

remedy. *Cure* is shorter.

remove. *Take away, take off, move, shift*.

remuneration. Euphemism for *pay, fee*.

render. Try *make, leave*.

repetition. Naturally, when you repeat something you use space and time that isn't strictly necessary. So you have to decide between brevity and the advantage of saying something over again. In general, it's more important to repeat. Saying it once and letting the reader forget is useless.

Don't shy away from repeating a word. It's much better to repeat than to use elegant variation with dragged-in synonyms.

replete. Fancy word for *full*.

reply. Bookish. Say *answer*.

reports. Start your reports with a brief summary of your conclusions and recommendations. Tell the gist first. Then use flashback and report on your study or research in the order in which you gathered the information. Tell how you went from ignorance to knowledge so that your reader can follow along easily. Arrive at your findings in the natural way. The order of a scientific paper is problem—procedure—findings. There's no better way.

represent. Say *be, stand for, show*. Usually *represent* is just a long word for *be*.

request. Don't say *request* when you mean *ask*. *Request* means you have a right to order someone else around: you probably don't mean that.

require. Try *need, call for, take*.

requirement. What is *needed, called for*.

research. Strictly speaking, research means laboratory or field work—finding facts by scientific observation, experiments or studying original documents. Much of what people call research is just search—getting information out of books and other printed sources. So don't be pompous about your research: of course you went and looked it up. So what? Does that make you a scientist?

reside. Say *live.*

residence. *House, apartment, address.*

residue. What's left.

resources. Try *means* or *money.*

respect. With *respect to:* say *on, about* or rewrite. *With respect to corporations, the law provides = the law says corporations . . .* etc.

respecting. Long preposition. Usually means *for.*

respectively. Nine times out of ten you can leave it out and nobody'll miss it. *The Ford, Chevy and Plymouth belonged to Tom, Dick and Harry respectively*—do you have to be as precise as all that?

response. Fancy word for *answer.*

responsibility. Long word that can often be spared. Try phrases with *in charge, up to, duty, job.*

restrict. *Limit, keep to, keep within.*

result. *With the result that = so that.* Time's Result: is a handy device.

resume. *Pick up, take up, go on.*

retain. Means *keep, hold on to.*

Rev. Don't use *Rev.* with the last name alone; say *Rev. Charles J. Brown* or *the Rev. Dr. Brown* or *the Rev. Mr. Brown* if he's not a doctor.

reveal. Business jargon for *show.*

reversal. Say *turn, turn back, twist, setback.*

revising. The time to be brief is when you're revising. The first draft should be written in an even flow, as if talking to your reader; then, when you revise, use your chance to cut out every extra word. Take out everything that doesn't seem right or necessary to your cold morning-after eye. Think twice before you put anything new *in.*

rhetorical questions. Go slow on rhetorical questions—that is, questions supposed to answer themselves. On the other hand, it's often a good idea to ask a question and then answer it right away. Why? Because that's one of the most effective devices there are.

rhythm. Write for the ear, not for the eye. If your writing wouldn't sound good when read aloud, then it's no good. Don't write sentences like this (from the *New York Times*): *That automatically created this fundamental issue in the committee hearings on confirming McCone's appointment: Do these responsibilities expand his functions, from those of administrator of the information-collecting operation of the C. I. A. and final arbiter of different evaluations among all the Government's intelligence units, to a policy-maker in fact?*

rise. Often sounds bookish. Try *get up.*

root words. Use root words, without prefixes and suffixes, as much as you can. *Jobs* is better than *responsibilities, boss* is better than *administrator.*

round. Write *year round, the other way round* (without apostrophe).

rudiments. *First steps, ABCs.*

rule and exception. Lawyers have a habit of starting with the exception and then going on to the rule, usually from the least common to the most common case. The normal way of thinking and writing is the other way round. Go from the most common rule to the second most common, and so on down, winding up with the exceptions.

S

s'. Write *Jones' house*, not *Jones's house*. It's shorter.

said. Don't worry about repeating *said* in written dialogue. It's much better and simpler than fancy synonyms like *muttered, remarked, explained, stated, exclaimed.* Use *said . . . said . . . said*; for what was said after a pause, use *add*; for answers to questions use *answered*.

And don't embellish *said* with adverbs either. Don't write *he said smilingly, she said wearily, he said hesitantly.* Just stick to *said*.

Never use the legal *said* (e.g. *said agreement*); use *the* or *that*.

sales letters. There's no point in being brief in a sales letter. Tests show that in mail-order selling long copy pays off. To get people to part with money, you have to use lots of words.

Don't fall for the argument that every business letter has to be a sales letter. That's only true in the sense that all letters should make a good impression. Be brief and to the point and you'll have added to the good will of your company.

salient. Try *high, striking*.

salutary. *Good* is good enough.

same. Don't use *same* for *the* or *that*; it's legal jargon.

sandwich method. Magazine article writers use the sandwich method, switching from layers of straight information to tasty anecdote filling and back again. Use the sandwich method whenever you're trying to teach or inform. Make your sandwiches overflow with entertaining filling.

sanguine. Bookish for *cheerful.*

satisfactory. *Good, good enough, fine,* OK.

save. Don't use *save* as a preposition meaning *except.*

say. Handy word for giving a quick example. *Say you're writing a collection letter . . . Your customer is, say, an old lady. . . .*

schism. Many people don't know it's pronounced SIZm. Avoid. Say *split.*

scientific papers. The standard way to write a scientific paper is this: (1) problem; (2) purpose (hypothesis to be tested); (3) procedure (of experiment); (4) findings; (5) conclusion and discussion. (In most current scientific journals, an abstract of each paper is printed on top.)

Follow this basic pattern in all reports and longer papers. Start with a brief summary, then go on to tell what you tried to do, how you went about it and what you found.

The main point about scientific papers is that other scientists must be able to repeat the experiments and observations if they want to check the author's work. Every scientific paper therefore must be something like an instruction manual for the reader. Each step must be specific and unmistakable.

Try to write everything like a scientific paper in that sense.

scrupulous. Overused for careful. *With scrupulous care = with great care.*

scrutiny, scrutinize. *Try check, study, look into.*

second novel. Second novels are often flops. Why? Because

second novel (*Contd.*)

an author who has been successful with a first novel, then sits down and tries to *think up* another one. This usually doesn't work because the first novel was autobiographical, and now he's out of material. Moral: Readers like something that comes out of experience; they don't care for what comes out of someone's mind.

secure. Don't use as a synonym for *get*.

seek. Bookish. Say *look for*.

seem. Don't say *seems* when you mean *is*. Don't hedge and pretend you don't mean what you say. *Our records seem to indicate* = *our records show*.

segment. *Part*.

select. Fancy word for *pick, choose*.

self-explanatory. *You will find the enclosed booklet self-explanatory*. No, he won't. Don't shirk the job of explaining it to him; he won't work his way through the small print and anyway, you have to tell him exactly what applies to his case and how.

semantics. Never mind semantics, the science of word meanings. Don't brood over the meanings of words. Deal with your subject, make it as clear as possible to your reader, and let the words come naturally.

Remember that dictionaries are made by studying the meanings of words used in various sources. Go ahead and write; let the scientists study *your* word usage.

semicolons. If you want to be brief, use semicolons. They're a signal to the reader that the pause between two related sentences is only half as long as that marked by a period. Break up your long sentences and use semicolons at the point where you broke your sentence in two. News magazines and digests are full of semicolons; follow their example.

sentence. Don't think of a sentence as a string of words between two periods. That's wrong; a sentence is a unit of speech, not of writing. It ends when your voice in speaking would mark a break. This break may be shown in writing by a period, a colon, a semicolon, a question mark, an exclamation point, a dash, or three dots plus a period if the sentence trails off.

If you change a period to a semicolon or colon, you haven't made one long sentence out of two; you just changed the punctuation between two sentences.

sentence fragments. English teachers insist you shouldn't use sentence fragments, e.g. *Or tomorrow.* But these so-called sentence fragments are usually fine sentences, common in conversational writing. Use them freely to give your writing an informal, colloquial touch. If you've never written such sentences before, start right now. Or tomorrow morning.

sentence length. In whatever you write, try to keep your average sentence length under 20 words (about two type-written lines on standard-size paper). News magazines and digests run to 15–17 words. Use colons and semicolons freely to mark your shorter sentences. As a rule of thumb, stick to one idea to a sentence.

Don't backslide into long sentences. Here's an example from *Time: A descendant of Mayflower Colonist William Brewster, ambitious Owen Brewster went into politics at 21, in a series of acrimonious campaigns climbed from state senator to Governor (1924–28), U. S. Representative (1934–40), and finally into the Senate, where as chairman of the War Investigating Committee he built a reputation as a relentless prosecutor of Democratic misdeeds but finally met his nemesis in the form of Financier Howard Hughes, who charged that Brewster had*

90

sentence length (*Contd.*)

attempted to blackmail him into surrendering control of Trans World Airlines—a charge that was never proved but that helped cost Brewster his Senate seat in the 1952 election and foiled his determined efforts to get an appointive job from the Eisenhower Administration. (115 words)

sentence order. The normal sentence order is subject—verb—object. It's always simplest to stick to that order.

sentence variety. Don't write a succession of sentences of the same type. Vary your approach. Nothing is as deadening as a string of *there is, there is, there is.*

The conventional way to get sentence variety is to start with a participle, a preposition, an adverb, etc., switching from one to the other in rotation. It's much better though to break the pattern of declarative statements and switch to a question, a brief answer and perhaps a short quote. Sometimes it helps to break a paragraph in two.

separate. Say *split, break, set off, set apart.*

shall and will, should and would. There's a fine distinction, mostly disregarded in the U.S. *I shall, I should, we shall, we should* sound bookish to most Americans; they say *I will, I would, we will, we would*—or rather, *I'll, I'd, we'll, we'd.* Stick to this usage in your writing; it'll probably come to you naturally anyway. And use contracted forms whenever you'd use them in talking.

shan't, shouldn't. When you do use *shall not* and *should not,* contract them too.

she'd, she'll, she's. More contractions, just as a reminder.

shirt-sleeve English. Here you sit in your shirt-sleeves, with your tie off, writing to a guy who's probably in *his* shirt-sleeves too, with *his* tie off. Why write as if both of you wore frock coats and striped pants?

short forms. Whenever there's a short form of a word, use it. Write *gas* for *gasoline,* TV for *television, math* for *mathematics, trig* for *trigonometry,* etc.

short items. People love to read short items in a newspaper or magazine. Don't blow up material that lends itself to one-paragraph writing. Serve it up in nuggets.

short stories. There are two kinds of short stories: the classic Maupassant—Kipling—Maugham type that has a plot and a point and can be retold as a brief anecdote, and the modern Chekhov—*New Yorker* type that gives the reader a "slice of life" and lets him draw his own conclusions. The conclusionless story has never been popular; people hate to be left in the air.

If you want to use stories in your writing, forget about Chekhov.

sibling. English has no word for brother-or-sister but that's no excuse for using an artificially revived sociologists' word.

significance. Use *meaning, point.*

signify. Say *mean.*

signs. Use signs for brevity; write %, $, &, +, etc. Give the marginal keys on your typewriter a workout. Sign language is quicker than words.

similarly. Another of those long connectives. Say *also, then, again, too* or leave out.

similes. Use similes only when they'd help your reader understand. A simile compares the thing you're writing about to something else; if the something else isn't thoroughly familiar to him, you'll distract your reader.

situated. Can often be left out. *The plant is situated in Columbus, Ohio = the plant is in Columbus, Ohio.*

situation. Using *situation* can become a bad habit. Watch

situation (*Contd.*)

this word. Avoid or replace it. *We don't want such a situation to develop = we don't want that to develop.*

slang. Slang is a special language used by a special group. Don't call a word *slang* if it's used and understood by everybody. If it's good enough for speaking, use it in writing.

slate. Headline jargon; avoid. Try *pick, plan, set.*

slay. Another headline word. Say *kill.*

sleep. A good night's sleep will improve your writing. Let it sit for a day. Tomorrow morning you'll cut it in half.

so. A good conjunction—better than *therefore, thus, consequently.* It's also a sort of pronoun, as in *I think so; do so.*

social science. If it's good writing, it's also apt to be good social science, with reports of observations and experiments that are clear and specific and can be repeated and checked by fellow scientists. If it's bad writing, it's probably social philosophy, essay-type speculation, armchair thinking.

socio-economic. There's no excuse for *socio-economic.* Rewrite.

soft news. Means stories that are interesting but not important. There's a trend toward more and more soft news in the papers. People would rather be entertained than learn something. This is one of the basic facts about writing.

somehow. Means you don't know how. Leave out.

someplace. More colloquial than *somewhere.* Use *someplace* whenever you'd say it.

somewhat. Don't modify and tone down everything you say. *This is a somewhat risky scheme*—well, is it risky or isn't it? Say *this is a risky scheme.*

sorry. Like *please* and *thank you,* use freely.

sources. If you give credit to all your sources, it'll naturally get in the way of your being brief. Play your sources down.

Abbreviate them, put them in parentheses, in footnotes, at the back. By all means give proper credit; but don't clutter up what you want to get across to your reader.

And don't think you have to give exact page references for every single phrase or half-sentence you quote; don't go foot-note-crazy.

space. By all means be brief, but don't try to save space—save your reader time. Be lavish with space. Use plenty of paragraphs, subheads, indentions, tabulations. Remember the effect of those ads that have a line or two of writing in the middle of a white, empty newspaper page. Make your writing stand out; be brief but effective.

specific. "Be specific" is the No. 1 rule of good writing.

specifically, more specifically. Don't use as a long conjunction. Say *for instance, for example,* or leave out.

speeches. A poor speaker reads haltingly from a prepared manuscript; a good speaker has a few notes and talks freely to his audience. The same way, a poor writer prepares his manuscript in mental isolation from his audience; a good writer assembles his notes and then sits down at his type-writer, talking freely to his readers.

speed of reading. To save your readers time, cut away words and speed the reading of those that are left. Here's how: (1) always use the shortest word that fits the purpose; (2) use as few commas as possible; (3) change periods to colons and semicolons; (4) use paragraphs and subheads for quick orientation on the page.

speed of writing. It usually doesn't take much time to do the routine thing, copy from your sources, and repeat the old stale phrases. It takes longer to be fresh, terse and to the point.

94

Anthony Trollope wrote his Victorian bestsellers at the steady rate of 1,000 words an hour (250 words each quarter hour) with a watch on his desk. (He wrote for three hours early in the morning, then went to the post office, where he had a full-time job.)

spelling. Don't use reformed spelling; it takes more time to read the unfamiliar spellings *nite, frate* and *thru* than *night, freight* and *through*.

split infinitive. Don't go out of your way to split an infinitive, but don't worry about it when you do. Your readers won't mind.

sports. Sports writing is a thing all by itself.

After spotting the New York Knickerbockers an early lead, the Syracuse Nationals regrouped and notched a 138–109 victory in a National Basketball Association game tonight.

The Nats were ahead by 34–32 at the end of the first quarter. They assured themselves of their 17th straight home-court victory over New York in a three-year span by taking a 76–48 half-time lead.

The Knicks' one mild rally came in the third quarter. After falling behind by 30 points, they ran off the next 11 points to make their deficit 87–68.

John Kerr ended that rally with two straight Syracuse baskets. The Nats' advantage grew to 124–85 with seven minutes remaining . . . etc.

Deadly stuff. Routine scores should be simply tabulated, like stock market quotations.

spouse. A strictly legal word. Say *husband* and *wife. Mate* is even worse.

spur. Headline word; avoid. Say *start, push*.

state. Don't use as synonym for *say*.

statement. *He made a statement* = *he said*.

statistics. Give your readers statistics only in very small doses. Use spot tables of, say, two columns with three items each. Round figures off; say 1 in 8, 2 in 3, etc. Beware of spuriously accurate percentages: if you ask 12 people and 7 say yes, don't say you got *an affirmative response of 58%*.

Tell about the average and the range. Mention interesting extremes. Remember that the median (halfway figure) is often a more meaningful average than the mean (sum total divided by number of items). The mean income of one millionaire and nine paupers is pretty good, but their median income is miserably low.

Be skeptical about your statistics. Your readers will be skeptical about them, and they may be right.

stellar. Formal word for the adjective *star*. Avoid.

stimulate. Try *bring, get, stir, raise*.

story. Newspapermen call all articles and features stories, and with good reason. For readers everything is a story, or it isn't worth reading. Think of whatever you're writing as a story.

stress. Stress in writing whatever you'd stress in speaking. Use underlining (italics in print). Use an occasional exclamation point. Or use a dash.

stylebooks. Different stylebooks give different rules for capitals, punctuation, compounds, hyphens, etc. If you want to be brief, choose a style that makes for fast reading. Use few capitals (write *street, ave.*, etc. in down style), use caps and lower case for headlines and titles, write compounds without hyphens (e.g. *byproduct, nonfiction*). If possible, use single quotation marks for ordinary quotes and double quotation marks for quotes within quotes, like the British.

subconscious. Freud insisted it should be *unconscious*, but most Americans say *subconscious*.

subheads. Use subheads freely. Underline them in typewritten copy and boldface them in print. Instead of subheads, you can also boldface the first phrases of key paragraphs.

Make your subheads real sub-headlines: tell the gist of what's coming. The reader should be able to get the whole story at a glance by just looking down the page and reading the subheads.

subject. Try to make the subject of the action you're talking about the grammatical subject of your sentence. If the grammatical subject is an abstract noun, rewrite the sentence so that the subject is a person. Example: *Comparison of the two report cards showed that Charlie had made much greater progress than Billy.* The grammatical subject of this sentence is the abstract noun *comparison*. But who is the real subject? Who did the comparing? Answer: you. Rewrite the sentence: *I compared the two report cards and found. . . .*

Don't use expressions like *the subject, the captioned, the above-named.* Cut through all that red tape and say *this.*

subjunctive. Use the subjunctive (*if I were*) whenever it comes naturally to you; when you'd use the indicative (*if I was*) in talking, use it in writing too.

submit. *Offer, put in.*

subordinate clauses. The more subordinate clauses, the harder to read. Break up your sentences and change subordinate clauses into separate sentences.

Don't write upside-down sentences with subordinate clauses that have more meat on them than the main clause, e.g.: *The plans were disclosed yesterday after Grayson Kirk, president of the university, rejected a student committee's request to turn*

97

the university-owned bookstore into a cooperative. If it's a main point in your story, it deserves a grammatical main clause.

subsequent to. Don't use. Say *after*.

subsequently. *Then.*

substance and form. Don't cling to the outward form of what you're writing; deal with the substance. If you use the annual report of your organization as a fund-raising device, don't make it too annual-reporty. Come out with it; never mind the formalities. Raise funds.

substantial, substantially. *Large, largely, much.*

substantiate. Try *prove*.

substitute. Try *replace* or *use instead*.

succumb. Don't use as a euphemism for *die*.

such. Lawyers often use *such* as a synonym for *that*. Don't.

success story. Success stories make good reading—that is, if they're failure-and-success stories, starting from nowhere and ending in a burst of glory. Readers like to identify themselves with the hero of a story, and it's easier if he isn't too successful to begin with.

Sufficient. Say *enough*.

suffixes. Cut down on suffixes. Keep your eyes open for *-ity, -ation, -ous, -al, -or, -ence, -ant, -ate, -ize*, etc. Use root words. Use active verbs.

suggestions. When you have a suggestion to offer, give the gist of your idea in your opening sentence. Then describe the problem and how you arrived at your solution.

When you accept a suggestion, say yes in your first sentence.

When you turn it down, say (regretfully) no in your first sentence. Don't lead up to a letdown.

summary. Everything can be summarized; it's up to you how much you decide to leave out.

Remember always that a summary belongs on top, not at the bottom. It took scientific journals half a century to pull their abstracts from the end of papers to the beginning. Scientists used to go through their journals with the fixed habit of reading the tail-end summaries first.

superfluous. Try *extra*.

superiority. Don't feel superior to the words you are using. Don't act as if it were painful to use the reader's language; don't write *a so-called sleeper* or put quotation marks around OK.

supernumerary. Again, say *extra*.

supersede. *Replace*.

superstitions. There are many superstitions about writing and grammar, e.g. that you shouldn't use a preposition at the end; split an infinitive; repeat a word within a paragraph; start a sentence with *and* or *but*. Don't go by half-remembered rules; write what comes natural to you.

supervision. Common long word. Rewrite. Try *in charge, run, at the head of*.

supply. Means *sell, give, lend, lease*—whatever fits.

suppose. Instead of starting a long *if* clause, start an independent sentence with *suppose*. Or, still shorter, start it with *say*.

supposition. Try *belief, thought, idea*.

survey. Often simply means *look over*.

surveys. Don't get pompous about surveys and polls. Statistics are fine when things can be measured and counted, but when it comes to people's thoughts about what they like or plan to do, percentages don't mean much. Your 73% yes answers are apt to include all shades of *yes, of course, certainly, sure, mm-hum, I s'pose so, I guess so*, plus any number of evasions, insincerities, misunderstandings and outright lies.

susceptible. Try *open to.*

suspense. Whenever you tell a story, anecdote, incident, case history, or use a verbal illustration, be sure to get all the suspense out of it that's in it. Don't spoil it by giving away the point. Keep it for the end. Let the reader ask what happened next; he'll read with more interest and understanding if he's curious to know how it all come out. You know all this, you say. OK; apply it.

sustain. Try *suffer, take.*

syllables. Count syllables in your writing to get a rough measure of readability. About 1½ syllables per word is a good average; 1.8 writing is heavy as lead.

If there are more than two words over two syllables on a typed line, look at it again. Try to get rid of the heavier words.

symbols. In a way, symbols are better than words. Numerals, for instance, are better understood than spelled-out figures. The same is true of the dollar sign and other commonly used symbols. Use a symbol rather than a word when you're sure your audience is familiar with it.

sympathy. The best letter of sympathy is one that tells specifically what you remember about the person who died. If you write *May I offer my sincere condolences at the occasion of your recent bereavement*, that's worse than nothing. But if you start *I remember the little game Uncle Paul played with Marjorie the last time he was at our house*, you're getting somewhere.

symptom. A *sign.*

syndrome. Several different *signs.*

100

synonyms. Don't use a synonym just because you don't want to repeat a word. Go ahead and repeat it, or use a pronoun. The hunt for synonyms will lead you to elegant variation and before you know it, you've written a string of pompous words you'd never use otherwise.

Don't use a book of synonyms or thesaurus. Stick to the words that come to you naturally.

synopsis. Write a synopsis of anything that runs to several pages and put it on top. Readers will be grateful.

synthesis. Bookish word. Try *one, whole, unit*.

T

tables. Long statistical tables are for reference, not for reading. If you expect readers not to skip tables, make them short (a couple of columns of three, four, five items). If you *have* to give them longer tables, explain what they show that's interesting. Point up averages, extremes, odd figures, important changes. Don't let your table speak for itself: it won't.

tact. Be tactful. It's good to be brief, but it's not good to be abrupt. Sometimes you need more words simply because they'll make your reader feel good.

Avoid all words that may annoy him. If you deal with a subject some of your readers may disagree with violently, take special pains to use neutral, courteous language. Say frankly *you may disagree with this* or *here's the case for the other side*.

take place. Don't use *take place* as a synonym for *happen*.

talk. Write as you talk. There's no reason why written language should be different from spoken language; it's just a record of what you'd say to your reader if he sat before you.

talking down. Don't talk down to your reader. Treat everybody with the same courtesy. Will Rogers said, "Everybody is ignorant, only on different subjects." Your reader may be ignorant of your subject, but he's bound to be smarter than you in other ways.

tape recorder. Tape-recorded interviews show what spoken language is really like. Study them to learn the kind of language that'll make your writing sound like live English.

teaching. Whenever you give readers information on a subject they don't know much about, you're teaching. Remember that; use the tools of teaching—repeat, summarize, drive home your points, go from the familiar to the unfamiliar, give illustrations. Make sure you leave your readers with more information than they had when they started.

teaser. TV plays start with a teaser—a dramatic scene that'll tempt viewers to watch the show. Start your writing the same way—begin with the most attention-getting point you've got.

technical terms. When you deal with a technical subject, you have to use technical terms. Explain them when you write for laymen; use them freely when you write for professionals. When your writing gets loaded down with many long, cumbersome technical terms, make doubly sure all the other words are as short and simple as you can make them.

technique. Rewrite the sentence and say *how to*.

telegraphic style. It's a good rule of thumb to write always as if you had to pay a dollar for each word. Cut out every word that doesn't help carry your message.

temporary. Long word meaning *short, for a time*.

102

tend. Bookish word. Try *be apt to, lean toward.*

tendency. *Has a tendency to* = *is apt to, often is, has a way of.*

tender. Try *offer, give, put in, send in.*

tentative. Say *trial.*

terminate. *End, stop.*

terms. *In terms of* is a clumsy preposition. Rewrite. *What this means in terms of our relations to Latin America* = *what this means for* (or *to*) *our relations to Latin America.*

textbooks. Textbooks are traditionally dull and pompous because they're written for teachers rather than students. The new programmed teaching-machine materials are quite different: they're scientifically designed so that students will learn step by step. Write instruction booklets, etc. the same way: remember there's no teacher on hand to explain what the book means. Everything has to be written so that the most ignorant learner will profit.

thank you. Don't try to vary *thank you* with *we are most grateful, we are much obliged, we deeply appreciate,* etc. Say *thank you* when you mean *thank you* and forget those other phrases.

thanking you in advance. Don't. Sounds as if you wanted to save yourself the job of saying it again.

that. *That* can often be left out, whether you use it as a relative pronoun or a conjunction. *Here's the material that I promised to send you* = *here's the material I promised to send you. I didn't know that you were sick* = *I didn't know you were sick.*

Which is heavier and more formal than *that;* whenever you can, change it to *that.* (See also **which.**)

That is also a handy demonstrative pronoun. Use it instead

103

of *the above, the aforementioned, the aforesaid, said, such, same,* etc.

that's. Use this contraction often. *That's why* is a good way to start a sentence or paragraph.

the. Leave out *the* whenever you can. Instead of *the same thing happened* you can say *same thing happened;* instead of *the next day it rained* say *next day it rained.* You can also leave out *the* before words referring to people by making them semi-titles: *movie star Bette Davis, owner Frank Porter, ex-husband Peter Green.* (A *Time* device; use with care.)

theme. Don't write your report, memo or letter like a theme. This isn't school, you know.

therapy. Try *help, cure, treatment.*

there are, there is. Watch out for sentences beginning with *there are* or *there is.* You're usually better off by rewriting them with strong active verbs.

there's. When you do write *there is,* make it *there's.*

thereafter. *Then, after that.*

thereby. *So, by it.*

therein. *In it.*

thereupon. *Then.*

thesaurus. Don't hunt for synonyms in a thesaurus. If you want a simpler synonym, try to think of what you'd *say.*

they, their, them. Use the plural pronoun freely after such words as *company, office, agency,* etc. *I got a letter from United Appliance today. They say. . . .*

they're, they'll, they've, they'd. More handy contractions.

thinking. Psychologists say the main secret of thinking and problem solving is to see the situation properly and focus on the key element. When you prepare for a writing job, shuffle

104

the material around in your mind until you see the right way to treat it and the key element to use for the lead.

third person. Don't use the third person when you can use the first or second person. Don't say *this company* when you mean *we*; don't say *the applicant* when you mean *you*.

this. A handy word; use it often. Say *this* instead of *the captioned, the subject, the matter in question,* etc.

though. Good casual adverb in such sentences as *this isn't always true though.* (Yes, you can leave out the comma.)

thus. Bookish. Say *so* or leave out. Often a colon works fine instead.

thwart. *Stop* will usually do.

time. *At this time = now. At that time = then.*

titles. Put your titles to work. Whenever possible, make them headlines, briefly telling the gist of your summary lead.

Don't use titles that simply name the general subject of your piece, e.g. *Great Contemporaries* or *Fire Insurance.* What about these subjects? What does your book or article say?

The worst titles are cryptic quotations or phrases that may mean anything. Secondhand bookstores are full of unsold copies of *Yesterday and Tomorrow, While the Sun Shines,* and *Hither and Yon.*

to be sure. Clumsy connective. Rewrite.

topic sentence. The conventional method of writing is to line up a string of topic sentences and expand each of them into a tidy paragraph. This makes for mechanical, lifeless writing. Never mind topic sentences. Get your mind filled up with your subject and then talk about it to your reader. Follow the natural line of thought.

trail. Headline word. Say *lose to, be last.*

transaction. Long word for *deal.*

transcend. Means *go beyond.*

transfer. Try *send, move, shift, hand over.*

transformation. Say *change.*

transitions. Every textbook on composition has a long chapter on transitions, training students to label paragraph after paragraph with *in addition, moreover, furthermore, nevertheless, on the other hand, finally.* Make an effort to write without these transitional crutches. Let your ideas follow each other in their natural order. If you feel you have to signal the reader, do it in the simplest possible way; say *then, next, and, now, so, but, too, though, now then, that's why.*

translation. When you write a memo, report, bulletin on a new regulation, procedure, policy, etc., face the fact that you're in the business of translation. It's your job to change the material from formal to informal English. Keep the difference between the two languages clearly in mind and go to work.

transmit. Means *send.*

transparent. Say *clear.*

transpire. Never use as a synonym for *happen.*

transport. Try *move, send, carry.*

transposing. A good copy editor does a lot of transposing. There are many places in a sentence where you can put a word or phrase, but only one of them is best for quick reading.

Go over your copy and transpose whatever needs transposing. Put the important words at the end; put the less important phrase in front.

treatment. *Handling* is simpler.

trite. It's better to be trite than pompous. *Dead as a doornail* is better than *deceased.*

truism. G. K. Chesterton said, "There is only one thing that requires real courage to say, and that is a truism."

106

truth. It's usually briefest and simplest to tell the truth. When you get stuck with something that seems impossible to phrase just right, stop and try to say exactly what you mean. Follow Mark Twain's advice, "When in doubt, tell the truth."

try and. In the last sentence, I wrote *try to*. If it's more natural to you to say *try and*, say *try and*.

type size. Don't punish your reader's eyes with anything under 8 points. Six-point footnotes are just as hard to read as 6-point text.

typewriter. Use the typewriter keys without letters as much as you can. Use figures, punctuation marks, capitals, quotation marks, dollar signs, underlining, parentheses, dashes. Use the question mark often. Paragraph freely. The most unreadable page is a solid block of words; the most inviting is broken up, irregular, full of various marks and symbols.

U

ultimately. *In the end.*

under separate cover. Usually unnecessary. Don't write *We are sending you a copy of the book under separate cover.* Of course you couldn't put it in with the letter.

under the circumstances. Some people insist on *in the circumstances*, but most of them don't care. It's shorter to say *what with all that* or *as it was*.

underdeveloped. Euphemism for *poor, backward*.

underlining. Show stress by underlining. Makes it easier to understand.

underprivileged. Silly euphemism for *poor, needy.*

undersigned. Don't say *the undersigned;* say *I.*

understand. Try *know, see, get, see why. I am sure you understand our position* sounds phony. Rewrite.

unintentionally. *By mistake.*

unity. If a piece of writing has unity, it's easier to read. Don't try to deal with two or more subjects at once. One thing at a time.

unless. A conditional negative is hard to take. *Unless this measure is approved = if this measure isn't approved.*

unless and until. A lawyer's phrase. *Until* by itself is just as good.

upon. You can always use *on.*

up to you. A handy idiom; use it.

usage. Have the courage of your own usage. Don't copy someone else's.

used to. Very handy idiom. English has no other way of saying that something used to happen in the past.

utilize. Long word for *use.*

V

vague on purpose. The only excuse for vagueness and long roundabout writing is that you want to hide the fact you're not saying anything. You have to be awfully good to hit just the right note.

variation. Don't use elegant variation: don't use synonyms just to avoid repetition. Repeat the word or use a pronoun.

verbal. Some people insist you should say *oral* when you mean by mouth, but everybody says *verbal*.

verbatim quotes. Quote people's own words; watch out for colorful and striking phrases. Put it down the way they said it.

verbs. Whenever you can, express your thoughts in verbs. Simple verbs meaning movements of the human body can say everything that is said by long abstract Latin-root nouns. Instead of *procrastination* say *put off*; instead of *dissemination* say *spread*; instead of *interruption* say *break*.

veritable. Usually unnecessary. *The place was a veritable shambles = the place was a shambles.*

very. Are you one of those people who overuse *very?* Try to strike out every *very* and see what happens. Usually it helps.

viable. Fancy word meaning *apt to live.*

vicinity. Neighborhood. *In this vicinity = around here.*

vie. Headline and Scrabble word. Say *compete.*

view. Overused. *In view of the fact that = since. With a view to = to. From the point of view of = for.*

virtually. Don't use as a synonym for *almost.*

virtue. *By virtue of = by, under.*

visualize. Long word for *see, imagine.*

vocabulary. You can't improve your writing by adding to your vocabulary. The more words you know, the greater the temptation to show off. Stick to words that come to you naturally and say what you mean in words you're thoroughly familiar with.

vocabulary (*Contd.*)

Try to *limit* your speaking and writing vocabulary. There should be lots of words you recognize in print but would never use yourself.

volume. Don't use *volume* as a synonym for *book*.

voluntary. Means *willing, on your own.*

W

W's. Always remember the 5 W's—who, what, when, where, why. Cover the 5 W's in your lead and pay attention to them throughout.

wasn't. A good contraction.

way. You don't need the apostrophe (*'way*) in *way down, way out, way back,* etc.

we. Use *we* and *us* only when you're talking on behalf of a group or organization. Don't use the editorial *we*—sounds stuffy. Don't use the educational, hospital, medical, dental *we: In the last chapter we talked about fractions. How are we feeling this morning? We haven't forgotten our diet, have we? Can we open a little wider?* Go easy on any kind of *we* and *us* that takes in the reader. Instead of *let's consider the implications* try *consider the implications.*

Don't use *we* or *us* when you mean Americans in general or mankind or whatnot. (*At this stage in the cold war we must all realize.* . . .) Don't act as if you were President of the United States. Don't make statements addressed to "every thinking American."

we're, we've, we'll. Handy contractions.

we are (remain), yours truly. Old-fashioned. End your letter with a period. Then add the complimentary close.

well-adjusted. Psychological jargon for *sane, well.*

well-nigh. Bookish. Say *almost, nearly.*

weren't. Another handy contraction.

what? Don't say *I beg your pardon?* instead of *What?* or *What did you say?* It's a genteelism.

what's. One more contraction.

what to do. The natural way to end a letter, memo, report.

when. When you have a choice, say *when* rather than *if.*

whence. Don't use. Say *from where.*

where. Don't say *where* when you mean *in a case where* (the legal *where*). Change it to *when. Where the taxpayer has filed a joint return* = *when the taxpayer has filed a joint return.*

where's. Contract whenever you can.

whereas. Famous legal pomposity. Avoid. Use *since.*

whether. When it's natural to say *if,* say *if.* Don't say *the question as to whether;* say *the question whether.*

which. *Which* is a heavier and more bookish pronoun than *that.* You have to use *which* in nonrestrictive (commenting) clauses like *I loved that book about the otter, which was a big bestseller last year* (the fact that it was a bestseller is just extra, thrown-in comment). But in restrictive (defining) clauses it is better to use *that,* e.g. *What was the name of the book about an otter that was a big bestseller?* (The fact that it was a bestseller is used to define the book.)

Most relative clauses are defining and should start with *that* rather than *which.* Hunt for *which* in your writing and change it to *that* whenever you can. Sometimes you can

111

leave out the pronoun altogether: *the book which I read last year* = *the book I read last year*.

When you do use *which*, put a comma before it.

whichever. An income-tax word (*20% of your adjusted gross income or $5,000, whichever is greater*). Don't torture your readers with mathematical puzzles. Say you have to pay such-and-such but if the other figure comes to more, pay *that*.

while. Usually it's better to make a compound sentence with *but* out of a *while* sentence. *While the committee hasn't yet reported on this bill, the White House is hopeful it will become law this year* = *the committee hasn't yet reported on this bill, but the White House* . . . etc.

white space. Sometimes it helps to leave some extra white space between two paragraphs to show the reader a sharp break in thought.

Use white space in writing as you would use an extra-long pause in speaking.

who'd, who'll, who's, who've. Common contractions.

whom. Even when it's grammatically super-correct, *whom* sounds bookish and unidiomatic. Most people don't use the word in speaking. Try to avoid it.

why. A handy word. Why? Because you can use it to change the pace. That's why.

-wise. Madison Avenue has been overdoing these words lately, but some of them are not bad for brief writing—*taxwise* and *costwise,* for instance.

wish. Don't say *wish* when you mean *want*.

wish to state, say, advise. Don't say you wish to do what you're doing anyway.

won't, wouldn't. Handy contractions.

would. Don't use *would* for hedging. *It would seem, it would appear*—you mean it is. OK, say so.

word length. Abstract, complex words are apt to run to three or more syllables. Use as few of them as possible. Try to keep an average word length of about 1½ syllables. Try to use not more than two words of three or more syllables on a typewritten line.

word origins. Words don't always mean what they used to mean or ought to mean. A nickel is made mostly of copper. Don't be fussy.

write as you talk. Write as you'd talk to your reader about the subject in hand. Test yourself by mentally throwing in *Joe* from time to time. *The prevailing causes of maladjustment, Joe, are socio-economic.* Would you *say* that to him?

writer. Don't say *the writer* when you mean *I.*

X

Xmas. Many religious people are bothered by this abbreviation. Avoid it. Say *Christmas.*

Y

yes. One of the handiest words in the language. Use it often in writing.

113

If your answer to an inquiry is yes, it's a good idea to make *yes* the first word of your letter.

yet. Don't use *yet* as a conjunction: *yet, on the other hand, we must not forget.* . . . Sounds bookish.

you, your. Keep a running conversation with your reader. Use the second-person pronoun whenever you can. Translate everything into *you* language. *This applies to citizens over 65 = if you're over 65, this applies to you. It must be remembered that = you must remember. Many people don't realize = perhaps you don't realize.*

Always write directly to *you*, the person you're trying to reach with your written message. Don't write in mental isolation; reach out to your reader.

you'd, you'll, you're, you've. Don't forget to contract.

youngster, youth. Don't use these bookish words for children and young people.

Z

zero. Avoid strings of zeros. Say *$5 million*, not *$5,000,000*.

Set in Linotype Electra with Durer
Format by Howard Burg
Manufactured by The Haddon Craftsmen, Inc.
Published by HARPER & ROW, INCORPORATED